GETTING UP & DOWN

MY 60 YEARS IN GOLF

Ken Venturi with Michael Arkush

TRIUMPH
BOOKS
CHICAGO

Library of Congress Cataloging-in-Publication Data
Venturi, Ken.
    Getting up & down : my 60 years in golf / Ken Venturi with Michael Arkush.
        p. cm.
    Includes index.
    ISBN 1-57243-606-9
        1. Venturi, Ken. 2. Golfers—United States—Biography. I. Arkush, Michael. II. Title.

GV964.V4A32 2004

2003066301

This book is available in quantity at special discounts for your group or organization. For further information, contact:
    Triumph Books
    601 South LaSalle Street
    Suite 500
    Chicago, Illinois 60605
    (312) 939-3330
    Fax (312) 663-3557

Printed in U.S.A.

ISBN 1-57243-606-9

Design by Amy Flammang-Carter

All photos courtesy of Ken Venturi except where indicated otherwise.

To my mother and father
For their unconditional love, patience, and understanding

CONTENTS

Foreword

MY FRIEND, KEN VENTURI

The date was June 2, 2002. Sunday's broadcast of the Kemper Open. The day Ken Venturi retired as the legendary CBS commentator and quietly stepped out of the millions of living rooms he had inhabited for 35 years. It was a day I had hoped would never come. But Kenny was ready to go.

"IN MANY WAYS, WE REGRETTED THIS DAY. WE HAD BEEN TALKING ABOUT IT SINCE LAST AUGUST AT THE PGA CHAMPIONSHIP WHEN KENNY SET THE DATE—JUNE 2. HE WANTED TO CLOSE OUT HIS CAREER IN WASHINGTON, THE CITY WHERE HE WON HIS NATIONAL OPEN IN 1964. WHERE HE DIRECTED THE UNITED STATES TO THE PRESIDENTS CUP VICTORY IN 2000. WE HAD JUNE 2 CIRCLED ON THE CALENDAR FOR A LONG TIME. AND WE KNEW THERE WOULD BE A LOT OF EMOTION."

—JIM NANTZ

Kenny has never lacked for emotion. Whether it was expressed that remarkable day at Congressional when he fulfilled a childhood dream, or the numerous times he openly wept on the air, Kenny was never afraid to let the viewer at home know exactly what he was thinking and feeling. Tom Pernice Jr. won the 2001 International at Castle Pines and Kenny broke down and cried when young Brooke Pernice, born with a disease that causes blindness, touched her daddy's face in search of his smile. In 1997, Americans grieved along with him as Kenny returned to the booth at the Greater Hartford Open, just weeks after his beloved wife Beau lost her battle with cancer. He was scared that day to go back on the air. He knew he would never make his way through the opening of the broadcast. And of course, he didn't, but that was fine. We all understood. He had allowed us to feel his pain. Many other times we got to share his joy.

> "THE UBIQUITOUS TRIBUTES, PLAYERS EXITING THE 18TH AT THE KEMPER WITH A TIP OF THE HAT, A SALUTE TO THE MAN THEY ALL GREW UP LISTENING TO. AN OUTPOURING OF AFFECTION."
> —JIM NANTZ

People forget, and I think even Kenny has never grasped, that his career as the lead golf analyst on CBS was more than three times longer than his competitive days on tour. His record as a player was exceedingly rewarding, yet far too short. Injuries ended that segment of his life. But what a blessing for all of us. That outpouring of affection that was showered upon Kenny at the

Kemper Open had nothing to do with his record as a golfer. It had everything to do with the deep appreciation for the years he served as the voice of reason for golf. The perfect spokesman for his sport. The welcome guest who came into our homes 20 weeks a year, shared his stories, and bared his soul.

> "AND I KNOW HOW THEY FEEL. I COULD HAVE NEVER IMAGINED AS A YOUNG BOY THAT I WOULD HAVE A CHANCE TO SIT IN A CHAIR NEXT TO YOU. I HAVE RELISHED THESE 17 YEARS TALKING TO YOU. TALKING LIFE WITH YOU. I HOPE YOU KNOW YOU WON'T BE SITTING IN THAT CHAIR ANY LONGER, BUT AS LONG AS I AM HERE, YOU WILL ALWAYS BE AT MY SIDE."
>
> —JIM NANTZ

> "YOU WILL ALWAYS BE IN MY THOUGHTS, JIMMY. I DON'T KNOW WHERE THE TIME WENT. IT'S UNBELIEVABLE."
>
> —KEN VENTURI

I feel blessed to have worked with him for as long as I did. Half his career. The time did fly. It seems like only yesterday when we first met. I called him Mr. Venturi for a number of years. Seemed like the right thing to do. At the 1986 Masters, I was making my way back to the CBS compound minutes after Jack Nicklaus had just won his sixth green jacket. Kenny came by in a cart and offered me a ride. He said, "How old are you, son?"

"I'm 26."

"Jimmy, you may one day be the first person to say they have broadcast 50 Masters, but I can promise you one thing, you will never live to see a greater day than this around here."

"Thank you, Mr. Venturi," I said with total awe given that he not only knew my name but would also see something in my ability to make such a forecast.

During that ride back to our headquarters, he had also said that Jack Nicklaus should have retired right there on the spot. Ken believed it would be the ultimate way to exit, winning The Masters at the age of 46.

For years after that he would talk about his friend Joe DiMaggio and how Joe always wanted to leave his playing days on his terms. His way.

> "YOUR DEAR FRIEND FRANK SINATRA SANG A SONG THAT EVERY TIME I HEAR IT, I THINK OF YOU. IT IS CALLED 'MY WAY.' YOU CERTAINLY DID IT YOUR WAY AND YOU'VE DONE IT BETTER THAN ANYONE EVER HAS."
>
> —JIM NANTZ

I think Kenny wanted to retire in 1997 after Beau's death. I urged him to come back. We had such a glorious time traveling the circuit together. Dinner every night. Stories of wisdom. I knew he was lonely when he wasn't out working. This gave him something to do. And he would be visiting his favorite places and pals back at Bel-Air, Cypress Point, and Burning Tree just to name a few. Man, do I miss those days.

But Kenny was ready for a new chapter in his life. In 2001, he had met a wonderful lady. He wanted to spend time with Kathleen. I was thrilled he had someone to share his life with. I often get asked if I stay in touch with Kenny. The answer, of course, is more than you can imagine. We still get together for dinners, talk on the phone, laugh at the little things. He'll always be a part of my life.

The video tribute we aired the day he said good-bye was filled with snapshots and clips from a very full life. One that has taken Kenny all over the world. One that has given him the chance to meet royalty and presidents. One that has given him the deepest reservoir of friendships and stories you could ever imagine. I had the piece end with "My Way." It all seemed to be playing in slow motion as I reflected on the man who had been like a surrogate father to me.

As the tribute ended, Kenny looked into the camera for one last pearl of wisdom before he would end his career at CBS.

> "THE GREATEST REWARD IN LIFE IS TO BE REMEMBERED. THANK YOU FOR REMEMBERING ME. MAY GOD BLESS YOU. AND MAY GOD BLESS AMERICA."
>
> —KEN VENTURI

We hugged. The cameras faded to black. There isn't a day that I don't remember him.

—Jim Nantz

PREFACE

When I elected in the spring of 2002 to put my story on paper, I made another important decision: I would tell the truth, at least as I remember it. That is how I have always lived my life, and I'm not about to change at this stage.

I realize, of course, that my particular version of the truth may offend others. But that was never my prime motivation. My prime motivation was to set the record straight—again, as I remember it. In the past I have kept quiet because of certain obligations, even when I felt my reputation had been harmed.

To be sure, after all these years it is not easy to recall every match, every shot, every putt. I have tried to piece together as many details as possible. To fill in any significant gaps, I have relied on old newspaper stories, which, I hope, offered an accurate and comprehensive account.

Except for my wife, Kathleen, I did not show the manuscript to anyone else, even my closest friends. I suppose I didn't want anyone to persuade me in even the slightest way from telling my side of the story. As such, I am grateful to former President George Bush for offering such a wonderful tribute to me on the back of the book. I only hope that the book lives up to his kind words.

ACKNOWLEDGMENTS

There isn't the time or space to thank all the people who have had such a profound impact on my life. In the pages that follow, it will become apparent how much their friendships will always mean to me. I never would have become the golfer—or the man—I became without their help.

I also want to express my gratitude to the numerous friends who are not mentioned in the manuscript, but have given me a tremendous amount of happiness over the years. They include: Andy Anderson, Elmer Angsman, Tom and Mel Bacon, Peter Bentley, Billy Black, Charlie Boswell, Robert Brownell, Gus Brigintino, George Burger, the Busby gang, Greg Carrano, Richard Casey, the Cranstons, Guido Cribari, Don Crouch, Bob Dailey, Dean and Gary, Myron Dees, Jug Eckert, Don Fernquest, Bill Gierisch, Walt Gilliam, Rudy Giuliani, Billy Hamilton, Jerry Hamilton, John Hass, Jim Herbert, Mickey Holden, Jerry Holley, Ralph Kiner, Don Klosterman, Bob Kniffen, Gus Kranites, Dick Krieger, Jack Leahey, Jack Lemmon, Dr. John Little, Tom Loss, Frank Mackle, Don McLaughlin, Jim McLean, Eddie Merrins,

Jack Mills, Emmy Moore Minister, Don Moonan, Admiral Moriority, Pat Moroney, Cardinal O'Connor, Tommy O'Leary, Bob Oligher, Danny O'Neil, Greg Orlen, Mike Palermo, Maria Paris, Joe Phillips, Frank Quadrelli, Frank Rizzo, Dave Rush, Dick Ryan, Tommy Sandom, Fran Santangelo, Chris Schenkel, Scott Schneider, Al Scoma, Bo and Leslie Sherwood, Lon Simmons, Eva Singer, Ken Skodacek, Dr. Jerry Slater, Dr. Jim Slater, Lou Spadia, Ralph Steinbarth, Ray Stoddard, Ovid Syler, Barry Terjesen, Hall Thompson, Bob Toski, Joe Turnesa Jr., Joe Veterano, the Vickers, Jerry Vroom, Don Wade, Rick Werner, and Rodney Wilson. I am very grateful as well, to the Beau Venturi Home and the gang at Pelican Bend.

A special thanks to Kathleen's children, Gina Palladino Bever, Debra Mancuso, and Joe Palladino, and my grandchildren, Andrew Venturi, Gianna Venturi, Peter Venturi, and Sara Venturi.

Above all else, I owe everything to the fans who followed me, first on the fairways, and then over the airwaves. It was not easy to give up competitive golf, but the support I've received in my second career has allowed me to savor every moment.

I am especially grateful to longtime sportswriter and author Michael Arkush, who was passionate about this book from the very beginning. Michael blended his knowledge of the game with a keen understanding of the story I wanted to tell. I have thoroughly enjoyed our frequent discussions, and cherish the friendship we have formed. Michael would like to express his appreciation to his fellow writers and to individuals in the golf industry who helped him track down numerous facts and statistics.

Finally, agent Jay Mandel of the William Morris Agency and editor Mike Emmerich deserve a lot of credit for their contributions to this project.

Chapter One

BACK TO THE FUTURE

It was cold and foggy, a typical San Francisco late afternoon in September of 1963. I walked into a bar on Geary Street, ready for another round of drinks and self-pity. My car was already there from the night before, another night I couldn't remember. Another night I was too drunk to drive home.

I couldn't get any lower. Another golf season was starting to wind down, and so, too, was my once-blossoming career. It hadn't been that long ago, after all, when the press anointed me as the next Ben Hogan, high praise I worked extremely hard to justify. I picked up two victories in 1957 (in only four months of eligibility), and four more in 1958. I even dressed for the part, donning Hogan's trademark white linen cap and steely expression.

But as the slump that began in the middle of 1961 grew worse and worse over the following two years, another, more sobering truth was emerging: I was definitely not the next Ben Hogan. I was, instead, a washed-up loser, closer to selling cars—my former line of work—than to winning them. My swing had vanished, along with my confidence.

My bank account, I feared, would be the next to disappear. In 1963, I finished 94th on the PGA Tour's money list, earning a paltry $3,848, not enough to pay my expenses. The companies that endorsed me weren't getting their money's worth. I knew it was only a matter of time before they cut me off and hooked up with the next new Hogan. I wouldn't be able to blame them. Nor would I blame tournament officials if they were to stop inviting me. I was only 32 years old. I felt like I was 62.

When did this nightmare begin? It's difficult to say. But, if I were to choose one turning point, the accident in Cleveland comes to mind. I was heading to the airport after playing in a corporate outing. A courtesy driver, assuming I was in a hurry, ran a red light. Another car broadsided us and sent me straight onto the driver's lap. At first, suffering no broken bones, I figured I was pretty fortunate. It could have been a lot worse. But, by the next morning, it *was* a lot worse. My back and ribs were killing me. Two long years would pass before I would be 100 percent again.

I should have taken time off to heal properly, which players would do today. But there were important contracts to fulfill and commitments to keep. I didn't possess the nest egg that the modern players can count on. Many are set for the rest of their lives. They don't have to make another putt. Others, if not as secure, can look forward to making good money well into their late fifties or early sixties with their mulligan, the Senior Tour. Players in my generation could look forward only to club pro jobs . . . if we were lucky.

By trying to compensate for the back problems, my swing became flatter, shorter, and faster. The quicker I could pull the trigger, the quicker the pain would be over. I no longer executed a big turn and release. I went from one of the prettiest swings in the game to one of the ugliest. Every time I teed it up, I waited for something bad to happen. I saw out-of-bounds stakes and water hazards as never before. I went from thinking about first place to thinking about making the cut.

One injury led to another. In 1962, while picking the ball out of the hole on the 10th green at a tournament in Palm Springs, I suddenly felt a sharp pain in my chest. I managed to finish the round, but was forced to withdraw the next day. The pain, later traced to the car accident, was excruciating. For weeks, I couldn't raise my right hand high enough to comb my hair. I tried every possible remedy—whirlpool baths, heating pads, cortisone shots. I would have tried a witch doctor if I thought it could work.

Nothing did. Finally, reluctantly, I took some time off, but when I returned, my game did not. Everyone was asking: "What's wrong with Venturi?" A few colleagues, such as Mike Souchak and Bob Rosburg, offered to help. But I was too proud, too stubborn, and too stupid to accept their help. I thought I knew all the answers. I knew nothing.

In 1962, I finished 66th on the money list. I had hit the bottom, I wrongly figured. I was about to go even lower, and I'm not referring to my scores.

What about my family? Weren't they able to provide critical emotional support during this painful period? I wish I could answer in the affirmative, but I can't. My wife, Conni, and I were not getting along. Conni was a loyal supporter as long as we were on top. But when my game started to go south, she wasn't so loyal anymore. She talked about looking elsewhere for security. "You're over the hill," Conni told me one unforgettable day. "There's nothing for me around here."

Our marriage was beginning to dissolve, though we wouldn't formally end it for years. We lived in a different time. Divorce was the last, not the first, resort. I turned instead to a friend, Mr. Jack Daniels. There was nowhere else to go.

I took a seat at the end of the bar, which hadn't opened yet. I didn't care. I wanted my familiar escape. I wanted another night to forget. Usually two, maybe three drinks, would do the job. But this time I was going to be served a lecture first. The bartender, Dave Marcelli, was an ex–University of San Francisco football player whom I had admired for years. Dave wasn't exactly the timid type.

"Ken, what the hell are you doing?" he said with an angry tone I had never detected from him. "What's the matter with you? Do you have any idea what you did to yourself last night? You have all the talent in the world and you've just been pissing it away. You're making a total wreck of yourself."

I didn't say a word. I stared straight ahead, afraid to look into his eyes. I didn't want to know what I had done to myself the night before.

"I believe in you and I trust you," Marcelli went on. "I want you to play well, and everyone wants you to play well."

I turned to look at him.

"Do you really believe what you're saying?" I finally said.

"I sure do," he said.

"Dave, I appreciate what you said," I told him. "I won't let you down." I wasn't kidding. I wasn't merely placating him so he would pour me another drink.

For some reason, what he stated so bluntly on that September afternoon in a San Francisco bar got through to me and my thick head in a way nothing else had before. Here was someone who totally believed in me, who was aware of what I had once been and could, with a lot of hard work, be once again. Instantly, I absorbed the painful truth of what he was saying: this is your last chance, Ken. Take it or leave it.

"Dave, give me a double Jack Daniels, please," I said. "What?" Dave responded, assuming that his passionate plea was being completely disregarded. I was going to leave it, apparently, and there was nothing he or anybody else could do about it. "Trust me," I assured him. "Give me a double Jack Daniels on the rocks."

For the next hour or so, I did more thinking than sipping. I can't remember exactly where my thoughts traveled, but they must have gone somewhere safe. Because, after I finished my one Jack Daniels, I leaned toward the edge of the counter and softly dropped the glass into the trash can. "Dave, I want to thank you for your advice," I said, "and I give you my word. I will not have another drink until I win again."

"I hope so, Ken," he said. "I'll be pulling for you."

I walked out of the bar and never went back. Even today, more than 40 years later, I will not drink Jack Daniels. I will ask for Crown Royal, and if they don't have it, I will order a glass of white wine. Jack Daniels reminds me of a past I don't care to ever resurrect.

I headed for home. For the entire drive, I kept talking to myself, realizing what a stupid jerk I had become. As Dave Marcelli put it, I had pissed away all my talent. I parked by the ocean. I don't know how long I stayed there. Might have been 15 minutes, might have been two hours. Who knows? All I recall is staring at the waves, pondering all that was lost.

I made one more stop that night. I went to California Golf Club, on the city's southern outskirts, where I had played so many rounds. With darkness approaching, few members were around. I walked toward the clubhouse, starting to map out what I was going to do the next day, the day after that, and the day after that. After a half hour, I returned to my car and slammed the door.

"Venturi," I told myself, "the game is on."

By 8:30 A.M. the following day, I was back at the club, hitting nothing but 9 irons and wedges. Since there was no driving range at that time, I picked out an area adjacent to the first fairway and used a shagger to retrieve the balls. Occasionally, I waited for groups to pass by.

My strategy was straightforward: rebuild my game, step by step, for as long as it would take. Luckily, the legendary Byron Nelson, the only instructor I ever worked with, was with me. Not in person, but in my mind. When I arrived home from the bar the night before, I had gone immediately to my file cabinet to retrieve the pages and pages of notes I took during our lessons in the early fifties.

More than a decade later, the lessons with Nelson made more sense than ever. As I executed each shot, I pretended that he was standing behind me. "Way to go," he'd say. "That's the Ken Venturi I know so well." Thank you, Byron.

I brought along his book, *Winning Golf*, with the inscription he wrote: "To Ken Venturi, my best and favorite pupil, hope you always have good fortune. Sincerely, Byron Nelson, 10-1-56." I kept walking back and forth between the book and my bag, reviewing the sections on the grip, the stance, the start of the backswing, and the downswing. I felt like I was studying for the bar exam.

The hours went by in a hurry. At noon each day I broke for lunch and then was back hitting balls by 1:00, going through bag after bag. As the days wore on, I moved up through every club in my bag, and then I hit 100 tee shots at the 10th tee. I occasionally played a quick round of 9, or perhaps 18, often by myself. By late afternoon I was exhausted, both physically and mentally, ready to quit for the day.

At that very moment, I would remember Roger Bannister. Bannister, the star runner who was the first person to break the four-minute mile barrier, in 1954, worked on his endurance by climbing this one steep hill over and over. When he thought he couldn't possibly climb it again, he climbed it one more time. For me, when I felt I couldn't hit another tee shot, I hit 20 more. When I was finally done, I would take a nap on the bench in the clubhouse. I often borrowed a couple of towels from the shower to prop my head up. Two or three hours later, I would wake up and leave. I stuck to that routine for several weeks.

The word was passed around to others at the club that nobody was to visit me on the range. The comeback I was attempting to pull off offered no guarantees. All my hard work could easily fall apart, and I would be selling cars again. The last thing I needed was the slightest bit of extra pressure. The only person allowed to watch me hit balls was past club president Bert Schroeder.

He knew enough to stay quiet.

Slowly, I started to see some progress. Not a tremendous amount, mind you, but enough to convince me that I could be competitive again on the PGA Tour. At least once a day, I holed a shot from more than 100 yards. I was shooting consistently in the 60s. My swing was returning to its longer, slower, more rhythmic tempo. The pain in my back and shoulders was gone. Most important, I was no longer afraid. I was looking at the middle of the fairways, not the out-of-bounds stakes or the water hazards. I couldn't remember the last time I felt that way. I also spent many hours on my short game. To get back to the top, I needed to learn how to score all over again. Golf is not like riding a bicycle.

In early October I was ready to emerge from isolation. To shoot well playing by myself or with a few friends in a safe, familiar environment like California Golf Club was one thing. To perform well on the road against the best players in the world with all the dollars and egos on the line was quite another. I wasn't sure if I was ready for such a pivotal test.

But I knew it was time to find out.

Well, if I was about to roll the dice on my golfing future, I couldn't have chosen a more appropriate place to start than Las Vegas, Nevada, site of the Sahara Invitational. However, when I went to register for the tournament, they told me my name was not on the list. A simple clerical mistake, I assumed, asking them to please check again. How could Ken Venturi not be on the list? I was a 10-time tour winner.

They did check again and there was no mistake. Actually, there was one mistake, and it was mine. I had failed to recognize that in most people's eyes I was, as Conni put it, "over the hill." I hadn't won a tournament in three long years. Who would pay their good money to watch me?

I went back to my locker, trying to sort out the ramifications of this latest, most humiliating rejection. All that work at California Golf Club suddenly seemed like a tremendous waste of time. The tour was moving on, and I feared I was left behind for good. But, while clearing out my locker, I was approached by the tournament officials.

"We are so sorry, Mr. Venturi," they told me. "We had your name, but it wasn't on the list. You are all set."

As apologetic as they tried to be, I was tempted to tell them exactly what they could do with their precious invite. I didn't need them, I figured, summoning the old arrogance I was known to display during my better days. There would be other tournaments that wouldn't dare to insult me like that. I would never play in Las Vegas again.

But the truth was, I did need them. I needed them desperately. I needed any opportunity to put my career back on track before it became too late. Stubborn pride was not something I could afford, not anymore.

So I politely accepted their apologies and started to put my stuff back in my locker. Only later did I find out the real reason they had changed their story. Several of my peers—Gardner Dickinson, Mike Souchak, Jay Hebert, and Lionel Hebert—rushed to my defense, threatening to withdraw from the tournament if I wasn't allowed to compete. I was quite moved. Can you imagine a similar stand being taken today? The game was less cutthroat in those days. We wanted to beat each other's brains out inside the ropes, but outside the ropes we were friends more than adversaries. I never forgot what they did for me.

I played fairly well that week, finishing 26th. More significantly, I made $675, which may not sound like a huge amount, but, believe me, for someone who had earned only about $3,000 for the whole year, it was like winning the lottery. With two kids at home to feed, every cent mattered. I also proved that I wasn't done, not yet anyway. Maybe I wasn't the new Hogan, but maybe, just maybe, I could be the old Venturi.

The 1963 season ended a few weeks later. As the game's reigning stars, Arnold Palmer (seven victories) and Jack Nicklaus (five, including The Masters and the PGA), finished first and second on the money list, I was left with a recurring thought: could I make it all the way back in 1964? I knew the challenge would be unlike anything I had ever encountered, but I knew it was one I was going to give everything I could to meet. The choice had been made, and there was no turning back.

I thought about Dave Marcelli and the empty Jack Daniels glass I dropped into the trash can. I had kept my word. I hadn't taken a single drop.

I thought about Ben Hogan, about how he had pulled off the most remarkable comeback ever in golf, and maybe in all of professional sports. If he could capture six major championships after a car accident that nearly killed him, then surely I could find a way to play well again. One thing was certain: I would have to work harder than ever, even harder than I did at California Golf Club. I would have to work as hard as Ben Hogan.

And I thought about a much earlier time, when I first fell in love with this wonderful game, and how it changed my life forever.

Chapter Two

MADE IN SAN FRANCISCO

Like many other Italians in his generation, my grandfather came to the United States in the early 1900s to create a better life for his family. About half of his relatives settled in New York, the other half in San Francisco. But, soon after arriving in California, with his wife expecting their fourth child, he became extremely ill. He was dying, but he had one final wish—to stay alive long enough to witness the birth of his last child.

He made it and saw the arrival of my father, Fredrico, who was then brought back to his mother. A few minutes later my grandfather was gone. His last wish fulfilled, he could make his final exit in peace. I never knew the cause of my grandfather's death, and I never bothered to ask. I knew better. My parents didn't talk much about personal matters.

I was born on May 15, 1931, in the heart of the Depression. Fortunately, with a lot of hard work, we didn't struggle as much as many other families. There was always enough food on the table and a roof over our heads. By watching my dad, I grew up with a tremendous amount of respect for a good work ethic, understanding that it remains the surest way to advance in any field. I remembered that lesson throughout my golf career. He went to work at about 6:30 in the morning, arrived home at about 7:00 P.M., and worked many Saturdays.

My dad sold net and twine on Fisherman's Wharf and up and down the California coast. Showing faith in his fellow man, he asked his bosses at C. J. Henry, a ship channelry company, if he could give the fishermen all the material they needed on credit. The company didn't share the same faith and was naturally concerned that the fishermen would never pay him back. No problem, my dad said. He would work the rest of his life, if necessary, until every single debt was covered. That didn't happen—the fishermen paid back every cent and never forgot his kindness. Years later, when many of them opened their own restaurants on the wharf, the word quickly spread: "When the Venturi kid comes in here, take care of him." Such treatment was passed on to the next generation when their sons, who were my age or older, took over ownership. I was always the Venturi "kid," well into my forties and fifties.

Even though we lived in the Mission District, a heavily Italian section of the city, my dad never spoke Italian around the house. My mom, Ethyl, whose family was from England and Ireland, couldn't understand it. As much as we made every effort to be fully assimilated Americans—my dad even shortened his name from Fredrico to Fred—we hung on to cherished family traditions from the old country. Every Sunday afternoon, we sat at a big, round table for a huge Italian feast. All the dishes were homemade and delicious. So delicious, in fact, that, years later, when I lived in an apartment at San Jose State, other students would line up outside, hoping to be invited in to sample the leftover lasagna and ravioli that my mom and grandmother gave me when I came home for the weekend.

I loved San Francisco in the early days. Our neighborhood was so safe that we never locked our front door. My mom wouldn't hesitate, as late as 9:00 or 10:00 at night, to walk a few blocks to the grocery store. I wouldn't suggest making the same walk today.

The only place I didn't feel safe was at school. I stammered, which made me a target for abuse from the bullies. People don't make fun of the blind or the deaf, but you're easy prey if you have trouble speaking.

I was constantly fighting with the kids who mimicked me. I got my licks in, all right, but if we had been in Las Vegas, I would have been declared the loser on each one of the judges' cards. I can't remember how many times my nose was busted. One guy would give me a shove, and I'd whack him back. Before I knew it, there were three or four others on top of me. No contest. I didn't tell my parents about the fights. I explained that I hit myself with some object or I came up with another excuse. They seemed to go along, but somewhere inside I must have known that they weren't fooled.

I wish I could say that only the kids at Aptos Junior High were cruel, but I can't. So was one teacher whom I will never forgive. I once asked her to not call on me to read aloud in class the next day. With my stammering, reading was always an ordeal, and the last thing I needed was more ridicule. From her reaction, I believed I would be spared, at least this one time. But when the time came, I found out differently.

"Who is the boy who told me he didn't want to read because he stammered?" she said in front of the whole class. Immediately, the other kids pointed to me. I couldn't believe what I was hearing. Nobody was on my side, I realized.

There was another incident that was even more humiliating. We were playing outside during recess when I took part in one of my usual scrapes. Suddenly a few of the bullies managed to remove my pants and hang them on a flagpole. When the bell rang, they rushed back inside while I went to retrieve my pants. Naturally, I was late to class, earning me an automatic trip to the vice principal's office.

When I arrived I told him the story, expecting to receive sympathy. There wasn't any. Instead he asked me for the names of the students who had committed this degrading act. When I didn't squeal, he resorted to the familiar punishment of that primitive era: he whipped me. The weapon of choice was a rubber hose, and, boy, did it ever sting. After I took my shirt off, he struck me eight times. Yet I still didn't squeal and I didn't cry. I just looked right at him.

"Get out of here," he finally said.

I'll never forget the look of anger on my mom's face that evening when she noticed the welts on my back. It was a look I never saw before and would never see again. When she brought me to school the next day, I was sure that she was going to kill the vice principal. I was in agony for days, but the pain was worth it. When the other kids discovered that I had not given them away, I gained their respect. From that day forward, they never mimicked me again.

Unfortunately, even after seeing a few speech therapists, the stammering remained as embarrassing as ever. I found out many years later that it may have been caused by switching at the age of five from left-handed to right-handed, which was fairly common at the time. Being left-handed was almost like being a leper. By the time I was eight, I could do everything right-handed.

My parents, to their credit, wouldn't bail me out when I got caught at the dinner table with certain words like "whhhich" or "wwwould." Their facial expressions and their comments never registered even the slightest sign of shame or disapproval. No matter how long it took, they waited until I got the word out. Only then did the conversation continue. With all the torment I endured at school, I can't imagine how I would have been able to cope if my parents weren't so tolerant. Their patience allowed me to recognize the value of self-reliance, of not waiting for somebody else to solve your problems, another early lesson I never forgot. If anything, in later years I became too adamant about refusing help. I sure could have used some during my slump in the early sixties.

When I was 12 or 13 years old, another therapist came to the school to observe me. The prognosis was not very favorable.

"I'm sorry," the therapist told my mom, "but your son is an incurable stammerer. He won't be able to speak right for the rest of his life."

I heard every single word, and when my mom and I arrived home, I started to cry. All I saw in front of me was a lifetime of humiliation. But my mom wasn't about to surrender. She wasn't the type. She sat with me on the steps and put her arms around me.

"Knowing you, you will overcome this," she said. "How do you plan on doing it?"

I stopped crying, as if the worst moment had suddenly, magically, passed, giving way to a new sense of determination I didn't realize I possessed. It took me a very long time to say the following words: "I'm going to take up the loneliest sport I can play, Mom. I'm going to be a golfer."

My pledge was not as ludicrous as it may have come across. During the previous three summers, I had worked as a caddie at San Francisco Golf Club, making 50 cents or sometimes a dollar per bag. I enjoyed being around the course, though I was more interested in three other sports: baseball, football, and basketball. I was a pretty decent baseball player, and, like many boys in the Bay Area, I idolized one of our own, Joe DiMaggio.

Being a caddie didn't necessarily mean I could play, as I discovered the first time I went a full 18 holes. My partner was Babe Stoltie, who owned a flower shop on Ocean Avenue. Borrowing a set of hickory shafts he stored in his garage, I played at Harding Park, a public course. My father, who usually shot around 80, gave me some last-minute instructions:

"You keep track of every shot you hit," he said, "and make sure every putt goes in the hole. But play fast." Play fast, I did, although you can't play too fast when you shoot 172. Yes, 172. Sixty years later, I can't recall a single shot from that round, but I do know that we never lost our spot and I counted everything, including whiffs. (With the 59 I recorded many years later, it's entirely possible I own two course records at Harding. Since that first round I've eagled every par-5, made 2s on every par-4 at least once, and aced three of the four par-3s. I never made a double eagle, at Harding, or anywhere else.)

My score didn't matter. What did matter was that I was forever hooked. Harding became my second home. Conveniently it was only about three miles from my real home. In the forties,

Harding was as highly rated as any private country club in the San Francisco area. You couldn't find a ball mark on the green or a poorly replaced divot. All of the profits went right back into the maintenance. (The course, sadly, went downhill during the seventies. Thankfully, a strong effort has been undertaken in recent years to restore its lost glory.)

I worked on my game for hours and hours on Harding's six-hole practice facility, trying to mimic the smooth, balanced swings I observed at San Francisco Golf Club. After school I rushed to the course to get dibs on one of the practice holes. Because we often had to wait an hour or two for a tee time, I hit thousands of putts, which paid off in the long run. I loved hitting balls, and I loved being alone, far away from any abuse.

The solitude afforded me a chance to work on my speech difficulties. There is definitely a correlation between the rhythm of speaking and the rhythm of the golf swing. I often pretended that I was an announcer. Little did I know.

"Ladies and gentlemen, Venturi only needs to pull off a safe approach shot and then 2-putt to win the United States Open, his first major title. He's about to hit, and there it is, a wonderful shot to within just five feet. The crowd is applauding the kid from San Francisco. He will win the Open." I was always fantasizing about the U.S. Open, never the PGA, the British Open, or even The Masters. On occasion people overheard me and probably thought I was nuts. "Who are you talking to?" they would ask. Soon there was improvement in both my game and my speech.

At times I played a few holes with my dad, although, after a long week of work, he preferred to relax with his buddies. We lived in a different era, before fathers bonded with their sons on the golf course. When we did hook up for a round together, I wanted to hit from the shorter tees, but he was never one to accept the easy way.

"You are playing back here," he said, pointing to the back tees.

"But, Dad," I pleaded, "I can't reach the greens from there."

"Good," he said, "you'll learn how to get up and down."

I wasn't too thrilled but, as was the case with many of his ideas, he knew exactly what he was doing. I developed a wonderful short game.

I sometimes caddied for my dad, which was fun. Well, most of the time. Once, on the first hole at Harding, he pushed his drive into the trees. Facing a blind second shot, he somehow found a wide enough opening to reach the green. "Good shot," I said, watching the ball get closer and closer and . . . "It went in the hole! It went in the hole!" I shouted. "Stop yelling," he said. I didn't stop. "It went in the hole!" Finally he had enough.

"Give me that bag, Son, and get out of here," he said. "You don't act like that on the golf course."

"I'm going to beat you someday," I vowed.

"Well, good, you just go out and work at it then," he said.

Again, he knew what he was doing. He knew I would work at it.

My dad was a very intense competitor. So intense that he never let me beat him. If I finished with a lower score over nine holes, the round didn't count.

"That's not a match," he would say. "It has to be a full 18 holes."

"Fine, 18 holes it is," I said, but then he would come up with another excuse. One afternoon when I was about 15 years old, I had him three holes down with three to play. I was finally going to do what I had promised long ago. Or maybe not.

"I've got to go make a phone call," he said, abruptly.

"You've got to finish the hole," I said. "Who do you have to call?"

"I can't tell you," he said.

He couldn't tell me because there was nobody to call. We didn't play any more matches after that—I was too good.

At 14, I won my flight in the city's junior competition at Lincoln Park. At 16, I was frequently breaking 70. I practiced all the time, even at home. My parents installed a living room carpet that was almost as slick as a putting green. We then settled into a nightly routine: Mom did the dishes, Dad read the paper, and I putted for another U.S. Open. I won a lot of Opens in my teens. The radio played my favorite mystery programs in the background: *Inner Sanctum*, *The Shadow*, and *Fibber McGee & Molly*. Those were good days.

There were times when I became too eager. I was trying out a new 3 wood in the house one day when I took a mighty rip—too mighty. I broke the plaster on the wall, but my mom didn't get mad. She never got mad, except for that incident with the vice principal.

"The wall can be fixed," she said. "More important, how did the swing feel?"

"Really good, Mom," I said. "Really good."

My mom was my most ardent cheerleader, boasting about my exploits to all her friends. She never missed an opportunity to say how much she cared about me. My dad's approach to parenting was a bit different. Like many fathers in his generation, the phrase, "I love you," didn't come naturally from his lips, but I always knew how he really felt. He, too, never missed an opportunity—an opportunity to teach me a valuable lesson.

Like the time I threatened to run away from home. My dad wasn't scared. He even helped me pack my suitcase. He escorted me down the stairs, opened the door, pushed me outside, and shut the door. I immediately rang the bell.

"Where am I going to go?" I said.

"I don't care," he answered. "You're leaving, aren't you?"

I rushed back inside.

"If you ever say you're leaving again," he warned, "you *will* be getting out of here."

Needless to say, the thought of leaving home never entered my mind again.

As stern as he could be, he never raised his voice or his hand to me. All he'd have to say was, "It will hurt me and your mother very bad if you do that," and that was more than enough. For years, before making any decision, I'd ask myself: would my mother and father be proud of me? I'm 72 years old and I still wonder.

My friends couldn't understand why I wouldn't even consider disobeying him. Being a rebel, after all, was a teenager's right, and I had the audacity not to exercise it. The most vivid example was when I asked my dad for a red motor scooter.

"You're not getting a motor scooter," he said. "I'll knock your head off. I don't want you to ever get on one of those. You understand?"

Well, a week or two later, I was walking toward Harding Park when a friend drove up and offered me a ride on his scooter. "I'll take you to the course," he said. "I'm going in that direction."

"No thanks," I said. "My dad told me not to get on a motor scooter," I explained. "I have to obey my dad."

"Don't be crazy," he said. "Your dad's not around. He won't know. You're stupid."

"Stupid or not," I said, "my dad told me no, and that's the way it is."

My friend shook his head and rode away. After walking about three blocks, I couldn't believe my eyes. The same friend was bleeding in the middle of the street. A woman ran a red light and cut off part of his leg. He was 16 years old. All I could think of was my dad.

After I told him the whole story, he began to realize it would be a smart idea for me to have my own wheels. Especially when I explained how a car would allow me to get in an extra hour or so of practice per day. For $125 he purchased a 1931 Model A Ford, which came, naturally, with very strict conditions. I was to drive the car only from home to school to the golf course to home. At night I could take it to Shaw's, the ice cream parlor where I worked until about 10:00.

"No joyrides," my dad warned me.

He didn't have to warn me. There were no joyrides in my life. For one thing, due to the stammering, I was way too shy to approach girls. I couldn't engage in a serious conversation. For another, I was already in love—with golf.

The first time I saw Byron Nelson in person was in 1946 during the San Francisco Open at the Olympic Club. I was mesmerized. I was struck by the way he hit the ball, the way he moved, the way he looked. As I began to take a picture of him getting ready to hit his approach to the fifth green, the two of us engaged in a little chat.

"Son, take that camera of yours," Nelson said, "and get back under the ropes with the rest of the gallery."

I did exactly what Mr. Nelson said. Riding away on my bicycle, I was so excited about meeting him that I dropped the camera on the ground and exposed the film. If only I had those pictures today.

"Byron Nelson spoke to me today, Mom," I said when I arrived home, explaining the whole sequence.

"That's not talking to you," she said.

But in the mind of an impressionable 14-year-old, it certainly was. I told her that when I grew up, I wanted to be just like Byron Nelson.

I started to read the papers more closely to keep track of Mr. Nelson's accomplishments. I had been, like so many others, especially awed by his remarkable run of 11 straight victories in 1945, the equivalent of Joe DiMaggio's 56-game hitting streak. If there is any record in professional golf that is untouchable, this is the one. Little did I imagine that someday this great man would become my great friend.

As for my own game, I was becoming more confident every day. One afternoon on Harding's putting green, I borrowed a Tommy Armour putter from my friend Doug Wadkins. I was making everything, so I told him I wanted to buy it.

"Fifteen dollars," Wadkins said.

"Fifteen dollars?" I said. "Are you crazy? You only paid $3.50 for it. Heck, you could buy a new one for $5."

"If you want the putter, it's $15," he answered.

I didn't have $15, so we agreed that I would pay him in regular installments. The putter would be mine. I then came up with a brilliant idea: a putting contest for 50 cents a hole. My reasoning was simple: there was only 50 cents in my pocket; if I were to lose the first hole, the contest would be over.

The Tommy Armour putter was still hot. I didn't lose the first hole, or the second, or the third, and so on. When I finished with Doug Wadkins, I gave him his $15, and walked away with a cool $11. I wish I could have putted like that on the tour. I was fearless. Wadkins sure wasn't thrilled when he found out I started with only 50 cents.

When I wasn't working on my game, I spent a lot of time at Cypress Point on the Monterey Peninsula, which to this day remains my favorite golf course in the world. My dad, on his way to see the fishermen along the coast, dropped me off at about 9:00 or 10:00 in the morning and usually didn't pick me up until it was pretty close to dark. That gave me plenty of time to caddie 36 holes and collect a nice chunk of change. I kept only a small portion of it and handed the rest to my mom.

Late in those afternoons, if nobody was playing, I would walk down to the tee at the famous 16th hole, with its gorgeous panoramic view of the Pacific Ocean. I brought golf magazines from the clubhouse to read about the exploits of Byron Nelson, Sam Snead, and Ben Hogan. Listening to the sound of the waves brushing against the coastline, I imagined someone reading about me someday.

Everyone at Cypress was always very nice to me. While I was waiting for my dad, the staff would bring me fried chicken from the kitchen and soft drinks from the pro shop. I vowed to repay them one day.

About 20 years later I did just that. Shortly after winning the Open, I drove to Cypress to see all the old guys. I figured they would still be there. You have to be crazy or die to ever leave

Cypress Point. When I arrived a few of the familiar caddies—Turk, Trixie, Joey—were in the caddie yard. Not much was going on. Most of the members would play after lunch.

"We thought you would forget about us," they said.

"I don't forget," I said. "But I want to repay you all for what you did for me."

I told them to get the chef. I then went to the trunk of my car and brought out a large box of Kentucky Fried Chicken. "Get the cooler in the back," I said, "but don't open it."

Everyone took a piece of chicken.

"I also want to repay you for all the soft drinks," I said, but I went one step further. I opened the cooler. Inside were six bottles of Dom Perignon. Kentucky Fried Chicken and Dom Perignon is not the kind of combination you see every day.

I felt I wanted to do something special, but I was really only doing what my dad always told me to do: "Never forget where you came from."

Chapter Three

BECOMING A CHAMPION

I loved golf in my early teens, but I wasn't prepared to make the type of single-minded commitment required to excel. I wasn't as devoted as the youngsters who pursue the game today, who get a swing coach before they get a driver's license. That whole thing is kind of absurd to me. Today's promising kids may hit it big someday, and I certainly hope they do, but I believe the price is too steep. You're not allowed to take a mulligan with your childhood.

I was playing more baseball than ever, manning center field, another perfect spot for a loner. I displayed enough talent, in fact, that Lefty O'Doul, the famous scout for the New York Yankees, offered me a chance to try out. I knew Lefty from Lake Merced Golf Club, where he was a member and I played in a few junior tournaments. Lefty was responsible for one of the most memorable days of my youth, when I met Joe DiMaggio at a restaurant on the wharf.

"Mr. DiMaggio, it is an honor. I admire you so much," I said, trying hard not to stammer.

"I've heard a lot about you," DiMaggio said. "You're a good golfer. You like baseball?"

"Yes," I said, "but I'll never be a Joe DiMaggio."

"Call me Joe," he said.

Call me Joe? Wow, I certainly had moved up in the world. Even now, I get a chill whenever I think of that first meeting, and it was more than 50 years ago. Soon afterward, Lefty invited me to Seals Stadium to shag fly balls for DiMaggio, who was getting ready for spring training. I was one lucky kid. Nearing the end of his career, he didn't like a lot of people around when he prepared. (Many years later Joe and I played quite a lot of golf together at the Presidio in San Francisco. Although I gave him a few tips, he was never better than a 16-handicapper. "You *meet* the ball, Joe," I said over and over to him. "You don't hit *at* the ball." His problem was that he never practiced. DiMaggio also wouldn't play in tournaments where there would be a gallery. "You're Joe DiMaggio," I told him. "Who cares what you shoot?" But he had a lot of pride.)

I also played football in high school, though my career ended rather abruptly. I caught a pass in practice one day and was knocked immediately to the ground. It knocked some sense into me.

"What are you doing, playing this game?" I thought to myself, writhing in pain. "I don't need this."

Well, I wasn't going to play this game anymore. I took my helmet off and left practice right away, never to put the pads on again. I didn't want to tell my dad. I was afraid he would think I was giving up.

"I wasn't going to tell you what to do, Son," he said, "but I'm really glad. You could have broken an arm or a leg."

If there was a single moment that crystallized everything for me, it came in 1948 when I flew to Boston to compete in the Hearst Championship, a very prestigious junior golf tournament. I stayed at the posh Copley Plaza near downtown. My room and my meals were paid for by the tournament officials, who also gave me several golf shirts. Now this is the way to live, I realized, not in the back of a crowded, smelly bus shuttling from one rinky-dink minor league town to another. I gave Lefty my answer about the tryout when I returned to San Francisco. I was done with baseball. (My first journey across the country to play golf, incidentally, had taken place a few weeks earlier. I took part in the inaugural U.S. Junior Amateur Championship in Ann Arbor, Michigan. After winning my first six matches, I lost in the finals to Dean Lind, 4 and 2, but what I remember most about that match was hurting my leg when I tripped off the 10th tee. Dean and I were all square at the time. I considered quitting but knew it wouldn't sit well with my dad. I dropped the next four holes.)

To live this new way, to stay at the Copley Plazas of the world, I had to work harder and harder on my game. Fortunately, I couldn't have been in a more ideal spot than San Francisco, with its choice of superb public tracks—Harding, Lincoln Park, Sharp Park. I was also given a junior membership at the Olympic Club. Because of the values that my dad instilled in me, I got along very well with the members. Many knew my dad and figured that any son of Fred Venturi's must be just as trustworthy.

No doubt I had plenty to learn, including how to lose. One especially painful experience came when, at the age of 14, I was beaten in a match at Lincoln Park, 7 and 5. To make matters worse,

I was convinced that my opponent had lied about his handicap; he belonged in a much lower flight. When the match concluded, I refused to go back to the clubhouse. I remained on the side of a little hill by the 13th green for some time, crying my eyes out. Finally, as dusk approached, my mom arrived to offer some solace.

"I know there are people who cheat," she said. "But don't ever cry in defeat. You may cry in victory but don't ever cry in defeat." I never forgot those words. I didn't cry after my heartbreaking loss in the 1956 Masters or after another loss at Augusta two years later. Only on one occasion, after Arnold Palmer birdied the last two holes to beat me by a stroke in the 1960 Masters, did I shed a few tears in defeat.

My emotions weren't the only thing I needed to keep under control. The other was my ego. Like many teenagers, it was enormous. Thank goodness there was someone around to straighten me out before I became completely insufferable. My dad, naturally.

I was 18 years old, fresh from capturing the 1950 San Francisco City Golf Championship over Bob Silvestri, becoming the youngest champion ever. For the first time, I believed I was destined to accomplish great things in the game of golf. I couldn't wait to share my newly discovered destiny with my dad.

"I was the best out there today, Dad," I boasted. "I'm so good, nobody can beat me." I had planned to make a simple declaration but it turned into a monologue. My dad stood silently, patiently, waiting for his opening.

"You finished?" he said.

"Yes, I believe so," I responded, convinced that I had made a compelling case.

"Let me tell you something," he said. "Son, when you're as good as you are, you can tell everybody. But when you get really good, Son, they'll tell you."

That shut me up in a hurry. I realized he was absolutely right, and I would try to never brag again.

Nonetheless, during my career, people assumed I was the most arrogant player they ever met. I sure gave them plenty of ammunition. When asked to predict who would win a particular tournament, my answer was always the same: "Me." I didn't really feel that way, of course, but issuing a one-word response was better than dealing with the humiliation of getting stuck in a long explanation such as: "There are a lot of talented players in the field. Any one of them could walk off with the championship." I was determined to keep my stammering a secret for as long as possible. (Years later, a picture of me flashing a Winston Churchill–like "V for victory" sign at The Masters appeared in the papers. "There goes that cocky Venturi again," the press wrote. What the press didn't write is that I had been asked if I wanted a Coke. The "V" was me holding up two fingers. I wanted two Cokes.)

Capturing the City Championship in 1950 *was* a big deal. I had won a series of junior titles in 1948 and '49—the San Francisco Interscholastic Championship, the Northern California Junior Championship, and the All-California Medal Play Championship. But winning the City, well, *that* was an accomplishment. I went head-to-head against the grown-ups in the country's oldest municipal golf tournament in front of thousands of people.

Many of the top amateurs in the country lived in the Bay Area, men with ordinary day jobs—police officers, firemen, insurance agents, dentists, schoolteachers—who played extraordinary golf. Because the most prestigious amateur events were typically staged on the East Coast, the premier California players, unable to afford the trip, never attracted the attention they deserved. No matter. I would have put our fields up against any amateur tournament anywhere.

In 1950, my first match in the City was against Martin Stanovich, who owned a mattress company in San Francisco. Stanovich, a stocky, short guy, possessed an unorthodox swing. Watching him stand over a golf ball, you would swear that he couldn't break 80 if he caught every break in the world. Looks aside, Stanovich was no slouch. He could reach the green from anywhere. Even so, my friends bet Stanovich, who loved to gamble, $3,500 that I would prevail.

Luckily, I wasn't aware of the wagering during the match. With that kind of pressure, I would have been a nervous wreck and might have choked. After the match, which I won 3 and 2, I found out about the bets. I asked Stanovich why he kept the gambling a secret the whole day, fully aware of the effect it might have had on me.

"That's not the way to go," he said. I'll always admire Martin Stanovich for knowing the right way to go.

My next opponent, Jim Molinari, the city champion in 1939, 1942, and 1947, wasn't quite as classy, to put it mildly. Molinari, a cop, was a strong man twice my age who assumed he could intimidate me. He assumed wrong.

"I'm in the junior championship," he said to a few of his friends while warming up on the range, loud enough for me to get the message. "I have to play a kid. This is a men's championship. This is not a tournament for a bunch of kids."

I kept hitting balls. I knew I couldn't answer him with my wit. I'd stammer and only make myself look worse. I needed to respond with a much more reliable weapon: my clubs. They didn't let me down. I birdied three of the first four holes to go 3 up. At the fifth tee, I approached Molinari.

"How do you like that, old man?" I said.

However, I was grateful for the tough, hard-nosed competitors like Jim Molinari. They stiffened my resolve, preparing me for the kind of gamesmanship I would come to recognize as routine behavior in the big leagues. When players such as Sam Snead tried to mess with my head, I thought back to Molinari. "Come on, boys, you're a bunch of amateurs," I said when they tried to rattle me. "You don't know what a needle is." Molinari was a fighter. He squared our match at the 10th, and again at the 14th. Fortunately, I won the 15th when he hit his drive out of bounds, halved the 16th, and clinched it at 17, winning 2 and 1.

Next up, I believe, was George Frazer, who had me 1 down heading into the 18th. Things appeared to get even worse when my approach finished 40 feet from the cup. But somehow I made the putt and prevailed on the first extra hole, where Frazer missed a six-footer and I sank a three-footer. I got by Einar Hanson in the following match, setting up a 36-hole final with Bob Silvestri, a navy veteran who had reportedly survived a sinking carrier in World War II. After what he had been through, it was pretty safe to assume that the man knew how to handle pressure.

Our match, before thousands of people, was a classic. I was 4 down after 18, and 3 down after 27. I needed to make my move fast, which thankfully I did. With three birdies in five holes, high-lighted by putts of 35 and 15 feet, we were all square. I gained the upper hand at the 35th hole, but Silvestri drilled a 31-footer at the last to extend the match. I was in huge trouble on the first extra hole, but Silvestri missed a seven-footer that would have won it. He would not have another chance. On the next hole, his drive came to rest in a divot hole, resulting in a bogey. I was the City champion. I cried, but there was nothing wrong with that. I was crying in victory.

Besides the boost in confidence, winning the City opened up all kinds of doors, none more significant than being introduced to Eddie Lowery. Lowery, best known for being Francis Ouimet's caddie for his remarkable victory in the historic 1913 U.S. Open at the Country Club in Brookline, was a big man in San Francisco. He owned one of the country's largest automobile dealerships and was considered a mentor to some of the most talented young golfers in town. (Ouimet, incidentally, eventually became my stockbroker. He was a warm, genuine man, unfazed by his place in the game's lore.)

"How would you like to play golf with me at the San Francisco Golf Club?" Lowery asked.

I probably gave the quickest reply in history. Along with the Olympic Club, the San Francisco Golf Club was the most highly regarded private course in the city. I was excited about going back to the place where I used to caddie. Only this time, someone would be carrying *my* bag.

I couldn't wait to show off to my former mates. Years earlier, I had boasted to them that one day something like this would happen. They laughed. They wouldn't be laughing now. I arrived at the club early and waited for Mr. Lowery. I wanted the moment to be as dramatic as possible.

"Let's go in," Lowery said. "Go ahead, Ken."

"No, Mr. Lowery," I said. "Please, you go first."

Lowery walked in with me right behind him. Before closing the door, I turned around one last time, looked at the caddies, and raised my arms in triumph. They went crazy. One of their own had made it.

Lowery and I hit it off from the start, forging a friendship that would remain strong for years and years. After my parents, he was the first person to take a serious interest in my future. This was long before entourages were a part of the scene. Every promising young player today has an entourage before he has acne. Lowery put me in touch with the right people, and with his guidance I was able to better manage my business affairs once I made it to the tour. I don't know how I could have succeeded without his help.

We played a lot of golf, often teaming together in $20 Nassaus ($20 for the front nine, $20 for the back nine, $20 overall). Lowery covered me until I could afford my own bankroll. I learned how to compete with something on the line, the perfect preparation for the PGA Tour. In those days, of course, the PGA Tour was the last thing on my mind. There was no money in professional golf. I loved the game and saw myself competing for many years, but only against the other top amateurs. My role model was Bobby Jones, the most notable amateur ever.

First I needed a college degree, which I pursued at San Jose State. I had enrolled in the fall of 1949 as a predental student. Was I excited about the prospect of putting my hands in other people's mouths? Not really. I was, however, excited about how a career as a dentist would provide me with the income and connections to stay active in amateur golf. Lawyers, doctors, dentists—many players in the City Championship and the California Amateur Championship enjoyed these stable, well-paying professions.

San Jose State was the ideal place for me. The school gave me a golf scholarship to cover my tuition, and the campus was only a little more than an hour from home, where I spent many weekends. I would leave San Francisco early Monday morning and make it to my classes in plenty of time. To pay for my room and board, I swept rooms at the college and waited on tables at the Alpha Phi sorority house. Not a bad gig, huh? Even if I was still too shy to ask any of the girls out, I wasn't too shy to look.

College opened up a whole new universe, one I was eager to explore. As a physical education major—I switched from predental when homework began to interfere with my golf practice—I took a class in boxing. I wasn't going to be the next Rocky Marciano, but I was able to handle myself. I was fascinated by the level of artistry, the dancing, the movement. Too bad I didn't possess those skills back in junior high. The bullies never would have put my pants on the flagpole. I also pledged at one of the fraternities, but I soon realized that the frat life, with all its partying and pageantry, wasn't the life for me. I cherished my privacy.

Though the school won the National Intercollegiate Golf Championship the year before I arrived, San Jose State didn't have the money to send the team to many of the major college tournaments. I thus missed the chance to test my abilities against other talented players across the country, but I didn't mind. There was plenty of formidable competition in the Bay Area. More important, San Jose Country Club offered me an honorary membership. Three days a week, I arrived at dawn to practice for a couple of hours before my 10:00 A.M. class. I was my own shagger. No matter what club I hit, the balls would run down this big slope in a line, making them very easy to retrieve. I hit so many balls, maybe a thousand a week, that when I left for the summer the club had to rebuild the practice tee.

I was a typical 18-year-old, assuming I could balance everything, but I quickly learned otherwise. One day, in Techniques of Teaching Football—a real class, I swear—the instructor, Bob Bronson, who was also the football coach, nailed me.

"Isn't that right, Mr. Venturi?" he asked.

"Is what right, Mr. Bronson?" I responded. "Sorry, I wasn't listening."

"I know you weren't," he said. "I saw you dozing."

Everyone laughed; I could offer no defense. But, much to my surprise, Mr. Bronson bailed me out.

"You all can laugh," he went on, "but on my way to school today, I drove by San Jose Country Club. I don't know what any of you were doing at dawn, but I saw Mr. Venturi hitting golf balls. If you guys want to be any good in whatever you do, you're going to have to make that kind of sacrifice."

Mr. Bronson smiled and looked back at me. "Mr. Venturi, no more dozing, right?"

"I promise, Mr. Bronson," I responded.

Even when I was awake, I didn't excel in the classroom. Fortunately, I received some assistance from Joe Zakarian, a senior who was on the golf team. He helped me map out a study schedule, similar to the discipline I had established on the range. Hitting the books was like anything else. One has to put in the time. For me, that was three hours a night. If it hadn't been for Zakarian, I would have received Cs or Ds instead of Bs and may not have had the opportunity to play college golf.

My practice on the range was also paying off. In four years at San Jose State, if I'm not mistaken, I lost only three interscholastic matches. In 1951, I captured the California Amateur at Pebble Beach, beating Bud Taylor, a dentist, in the finals, 7 and 6. The win was every bit as satisfying as my victory in the City Championship. There weren't any amateur golfers in the state more accomplished than Bud Taylor, who had enough game to make it as a professional.

In January of 1952 I returned to Pebble Beach for an even more imposing challenge. My opponents this time wouldn't be dentists, insurance agents, or police officers—they would be the best players in the world.

It all started, innocently enough, one day in a political science class. There was a phone call for me, the teacher said, from a Mr. Bing Crosby.

"Tell him I'm busy," I joked, as everyone laughed.

Someone was obviously trying to pull a fast one on me.

"They told me they really think it's Bing Crosby," the teacher insisted.

I went to the office. Fine, I figured, I'll play along. I picked up the phone and said hello.

"Ken, hi, this is Bing Crosby," the familiar voice said on the other end. Nobody was pulling a fast one. "I hate to call you this late [the tournament was to start the next day], but I was wondering if you could do me a favor," he said. "One of my amateurs has dropped out, and I don't have anybody to replace him. I wonder if you would like to play in my tournament. Can you come down?"

Can you come down? I answered Crosby quicker than I answered Eddie Lowery when he took me to San Francisco Golf Club. Crosby even put me up in his house by the 13th hole, complete with my own room, a TV set, a refrigerator, everything a college kid could want.

For my first time in competition against the pros, I fared pretty well. I wasn't intimidated. Thinking of my dad, I didn't tell anyone how good I was. I tried to show them. Even so, pursuing a career in professional golf was still not on my radar screen. I was preoccupied with trying to recapture the City Golf Championship, which I had been unable to successfully defend in 1951.

After winning a few matches, I found myself in the semis against Silvestri, the man I had defeated for the title two years earlier. A huge crowd showed up for our rematch.

I only wish I had shown up. With six holes left in the 36-hole match, I was 5 down. Silvestri, who chipped in from 60 feet for an eagle at the 30th hole, was playing superb golf. All he had to do was keep breathing and he was headed to the finals, which made what happened next hard to believe.

After knocking a birdie putt at the 31st hole to within gimme range, I nonchalantly raked it back with my putter, the ball rolling a few inches. I picked it up, assuming my par was conceded. I had won the hole.

"We didn't give you that putt," said Silvestri's caddie.

"That's crazy," I said at the 14th tee, with no gallery around us. "Don't blow it. You've got me 4 down."

"I'm calling it on you," he said.

"You're making a big mistake," I countered. "If you're going to call it on me, then you've got 15 clubs in your bag," I said.

They went into shock.

"When did you notice that?" they asked.

"On the fifth hole," I said.

"Why didn't you call it?" they asked.

"I might have if it were the first hole," I said, "but I didn't want to win like that." Silvestri, alarmed that his blunder might cost him an easy victory, started to take the extra club, a driver, out of the bag.

"Don't do that," I said. "It will be obvious. Everyone will know."

He claimed it was a mere oversight. Oversight or not, I said, the rule is clear.

So we played on, Silvestri clinching the match—for now, at least—on the 32nd hole with 5 and 4. Along with a few officials, Silvestri and I immediately convened in the women's lounge to discuss the matter. My dad, the tournament director, excused himself. "My son will make his decision," he said.

In the end, I decided not to accept the disqualification, which was within my rights. By doing so, the tournament committee was able to exercise its power to waive, in exceptional cases, the penalty of disqualification. Silvestri was spared.

Why didn't I accept the disqualification? That's easy. To me, it wasn't the right way to win. Fourteen or fifteen clubs, he was the better player that day.

About six months later, I was at the Seattle Golf Club for the United States Amateur. I was not playing well. In my opening match against Arnold Blum, I was 3 down with four to play. Here was my big opportunity to make a statement on the national level, and I was making one, all right, only not one worth repeating. I bounced back with three straight birdies to even the match, but Blum birdied 18 to close it out. I walked off the green, dejected over such a premature exit.

I didn't stay dejected for long. Instead, Lowery introduced me to his special guest.

"I'd like you to meet Byron Nelson," he said.

I was stunned. I hadn't known that Byron Nelson was in the gallery. That's how focused I was. Just like when I met DiMaggio, I was praying I wouldn't stammer. I somehow held it together.

"This is quite an honor, Mr. Nelson," I said. "I wish I could have played better today."

"You played very well today, Ken," he said. "How would you like to work with me? Eddie and I are going back to San Francisco and wondered whether you might like to join us for a round of golf tomorrow."

"Oh my gosh, Mr. Nelson," I said. "I sure would."

The only trouble was getting to San Francisco in time. While Nelson and Lowery went to the airport, my only mode of transportation was a 1942 Buick Roadster. Seattle to San Francisco was a long way, and it became even longer when my car got a flat tire. I began to fear the worst: Lowery and Nelson enjoying a pleasant round at San Francisco Golf Club, with me, the irresponsible 21-year-old, stuck on a highway in the middle of nowhere, squandering the opportunity of a lifetime. Fortunately, the fear subsided as I quickly fixed the flat and drove through the day, arriving in San Francisco in the late evening. I would have hitchhiked, if necessary.

We met at the club for lunch and then headed to the first tee.

"Ken," Mr. Nelson said, "I'm not going to give you any lessons. I'm just going to watch you very closely."

The pressure was on like never before. Surprisingly, I played very well. The only comments I heard all afternoon from Mr. Nelson were: "Good shot, Ken," or "Well hit, Ken," or "Good putt, Ken." I finished with a 66, confident there was nothing the great Nelson could tell the great Venturi. We went to the clubhouse for some soft drinks, and I waited for the accolades.

None were coming, and I became impatient.

"Mr. Nelson, what did you think of my play?" I asked, smugly.

"Ken, that was a good round," he said, slowly, carefully. "I'll be here three or four days and there are about seven or eight things we've got to work on to make you a good player. I'll meet you out here tomorrow at 9:00 A.M."

Seven or eight things? To make me a good player? I couldn't believe it. I was already a good player. With all due respect to Mr. Nelson, what golfer did he think he was watching out there, anyway? Certainly not me. Needless to say, I kept those feelings to myself. I wasn't that stupid.

"I'll be there," I said.

The next three days were the most productive of my entire career. For someone who had never taken a formal golf lesson—I received only a few tips here and there—working with Nelson was quite an eye-opener. He turned me from being a player who used his hands too much into one in which my hands, shoulder, and body moved in one fluid motion, a swing that would work more consistently, especially in the heat of competition. He worked on my positioning, timing, balance, grip, and weight distribution. Nelson was a sensitive instructor, yet he knew when to be stern.

"I know you're going back soon to defend your title in the State Amateur," he said. "But I've got to impress on you the fact that you've got to stay with what we're doing. If you go back to your old swing, even for a few holes, you'll do it all the time when the pressure comes, and you will have learned nothing."

"I promise you that I will not revert back," I told him.

"You're a good mimic," he added. "But I don't want you mimicking. That's not how you'll learn."

I stuck to my promise and, not surprisingly, was unable to repeat as champion. I didn't mind. What mattered more was that I was growing more comfortable each day with my new swing. I was building a swing that would last. Working with Nelson inspired me to become a true shotmaker. Before his coaching, I had focused more attention on my short game.

In 1953 the two of us took off to play in a series of exhibitions up and down the West Coast. We talked little during the round but afterward went over the strategy behind almost every shot. With my swing under control, the next priority was to refine my golf management skills. There was nobody better to teach golf management than Byron Nelson. "Don't try to take it over the bunker unless it's a necessity," he said, or "You want to come in toward the center of the green and maybe cut it," or "What about choking down a 7 iron instead to lower the ball flight?" I took tons of notes, the same notes I would refer to during my comeback attempt at California Golf Club in 1963. I also developed the routine of evaluating each round to determine my mistakes, mental or physical.

I learned a tremendous amount about how to play with class. Nobody had more than Byron Nelson. For instance, before our rounds, he always asked for the course record and who owned it. I once asked him why.

"If it's owned by the home pro," he told me, "you never break it. Remember, he lives there and you are only visiting." (I never forgot what Nelson said. In the late seventies, during a recreational round at the challenging Westchester Country Club, the current site of the tour's Buick Classic, I went eagle, par, birdie, eagle, birdie, hole in one. I suddenly realized that I could break the course record with a par. I proceeded to intentionally take a double-bogey 7 on the final hole to keep the prior record intact.)

I never liked to lose, but there is little doubt that my loss to Arnold Blum in the 1952 U.S. Amateur was the best loss of my career. Otherwise, I wouldn't have played with Nelson in San Francisco. I don't even want to think about how I would have managed without his influence in my game and in my life.

With Eddie Lowery and Byron Nelson on board—I guess I did have an entourage—I geared up for my senior year at San Jose State. Soon enough, we would add one more to the group.

Chapter Four

MARRIAGE, THE MASTERS, AND THE MILITARY

I saw her for the first time on campus in September of 1952. "Wow, that's a good-looking chick," I told a friend. Of course, meeting good-looking chicks wasn't exactly my forte. I was 21 and had never had a serious girlfriend.

This time would be different, I told myself. I introduced myself, forgetting about my stammer. I can't recall the specifics of our conversation, but I must have done pretty well because we had a date for the following night to see a movie. For weeks, as our romance started to bloom, I assumed it was my boldness that set the tone. Wrong again, Venturi. Conni MacLean, as she later confessed, had been interested in me for about a year, ever since she saw me participate in the 1951 California Amateur at Pebble Beach. "I'm going to marry him," she told her mother.

During our courtship my game remained on fire. I captured my second City Championship, the Northern California Amateur, and a series of other significant events. Winning the City was extremely rewarding, especially in the wake of the controversy generated by the Silvestri match in 1952. After outdueling Art Schroeder, a friend since grammar school, I squared off in the finals against Art Linhares, a policeman on the Daly City force. I was running out of energy, having gone through five grueling rounds of the Northern California Intercollegiate Championship at Stanford, where I prevailed on the 19th hole against Fred Brown.

With a respectable 69, I was 1 up after the morning round. I should have been further ahead, but Linhares was getting it up and down from everywhere. On the first hole of the afternoon 18, he lined up for a very short putt. I thought for a moment about giving it to him and was actually starting to feel a little ashamed of myself . . . until he missed it. Linhares wasn't the same player after that. I won the match, 8 and 7.

My successes earned me a place on the 1953 United States Walker Cup squad, which pitted the nation's top amateurs against a squad from Great Britain and Ireland. My teammates included Charles Coe, Gene Littler, Don Cherry, Dick Chapman, Sam Urzetta, Jack Westland, James Jackson, William Campbell, and Harvie Ward. In the fall of 1953, we squared off against the Brits at the Kittansett Club in Massachusetts. The big question was: which twosome would go against their number one pair, Joe Carr and Ronnie White?

"Are there any two players in this room who think they'd like to have them?" Charley Yates, our captain, asked.

Sam Urzetta and I stood up without hesitation. "We'll take them," we said.

We took them, all right, handing the Carr-White duo their first defeat ever in team competition, 6 and 4, as the U.S. squad prevailed 9 and 3.

The Walker Cup experience offered me a chance to renew my growing friendship with Harvie Ward, whom I had met a year earlier at the Americas Cup. That tournament matched a team from the United States against players from Canada and Mexico. I discovered that Ward was as cocky as I was when we were paired together in the alternate shot format. "Boy, you get on the green, don't you be lagging. You understand me? I can make anything coming back." He wasn't kidding. On the first hole I took a solid rip at a 20-footer, sending it five or six feet past the hole. Ward walked up nonchalantly and rammed it into the cup. We were untouchable that week, winning one match 13 and 12 and another 10 and 9. Ward and I were sitting on the veranda when another twosome from our team went by on their way to the 10th tee.

"What are you guys doing?" they wondered.

"We're all through," we told them.

At the Walker Cup, I dispatched my singles opponent, James Wilson, winning 9 and 8. That 1953 Walker Cup team was talented enough to compete with the Ryder Cup squad, which included Sam Snead, Cary Middlecoff, Jackie Burke, and Lloyd Mangrum. I made that very suggestion, in fact, but it was a no-win situation for the pros. A loss to a group of amateurs would have looked bad.

I was a college graduate ready to enter the real world. After giving up the idea of dentistry, I needed a profession.

Enter Eddie Lowery to the rescue. Lowery put me to work at his Lincoln-Mercury dealership. I was no Byron Nelson, but in Northern California golf circles, I was a fairly prominent name, which is why Lowery brought me aboard. He was certainly fond of me, but, like any shrewd businessman, he was also fond of the bottom line. Everybody who played golf in the Bay Area purchased cars from our dealership. The setup was ideal for me: I sold cars in the morning and played golf in the afternoon. The office was close to California Golf Club, where the agency paid the entire $500 membership fee. Everything was going well.

Well, almost everything. In early 1954 I received a letter in the mail from Uncle Sam, and it wasn't a graduation card. I knew a draft notice might be coming, but that didn't lessen its impact. I'm almost ashamed to admit that, at first, I wasn't too thrilled with the idea of serving in our armed forces. I was quite concerned about the effect the time away from competition would have on my golf game. Besides, there was one country I wasn't too crazy about visiting. They called it Korea.

I was inducted into the army in late January and then went to Fort Ord near Monterey for eight weeks of basic training. There was the standard regimen—the shaved head, the early-morning reveille, and the strict drill sergeant. All in all, I managed pretty well. The eight weeks were going by faster than I had imagined they would. With only one week of basic left I was given a leave by Major General Robert McClure, primarily so that I could take a trip back East. My main destination was a town in Georgia. The name: Augusta.

On the way I stopped in Miami to play a few rounds with Harvie Ward, also bound for The Masters. One afternoon we found ourselves in a money game.

"How about playing for 1, 1, and 2?" our two opponents said.

That seemed reasonable enough, I thought. The most we each could lose was probably about $10. Harvie and I could afford that.

But at the 16th tee we learned that the stakes were slightly different.

"You got us out for $400. We'd like to press you for $200," they said. We suddenly realized we had been off by a few zeroes. We were playing for $100, $100, and $200!

"We need you to give us one shot over the last three holes," they continued.

"OK," we said, figuring that, at the very least, we'd still earn $200, and maybe even $600.

We gave them the one shot, and we were still able to halve the last three holes, winning $400 apiece, or what I'd make in about six months in the service. I'll always remember Harvie and me riding down a Miami street in a friend's brand-new yellow Corvette convertible, drinking beers, two friends on a new adventure.

My new adventures were only beginning. A few days later I arrived at Augusta National. I had never seen a more beautiful place. Because I couldn't be certain when, or if, I'd ever be back, I was determined to savor every second of this experience. I had qualified through my participation on the Walker Cup team, but how many more Walker Cups would I make? Little did I know I was beginning a special relationship, and not only with the golf course.

Playing with Harvie Ward, I shot a 76 in the first round, but it is Friday's second round that I will always remember. I was having dinner on Thursday night with Eddie Lowery and Bill Danforth, a member of the club, when they casually asked who I would like to be paired with the following day.

"Ben Hogan," I said, without any hesitation. Fat chance that will happen, I figured.

Danforth turned around. "Cliff," he said across the room to tournament chairman Cliff Roberts, "pair Ken with Ben Hogan tomorrow."

Just like that, I got my wish. Danforth possessed that much clout.

I was in shock. Not even a full year had passed since I followed Hogan for the last 36 holes at Oakmont Country Club in western Pennsylvania, when he won the 1953 U.S. Open. It was his second of three major victories in what was to go down, arguably, as the greatest year a professional golfer has ever enjoyed. I decided to stick around after missing the cut, and I'm glad I did. (In the 1953 Open, I birdied the first hole. "This course isn't so hard," I said to myself. "I'm really good." On the second hole, I realized I wasn't as good as I thought. My birdie putt from about 20 feet kept going and going and going . . . right off the green. I finished with a double-bogey six, and that was that.)

I learned so much that day watching Hogan manage his game. Now it was my turn to manage—my emotions. Here I was, Private Ken Venturi, on a leave from the United States Army, paired with the legendary Ben Hogan in the second round of The Masters! And I thought there was pressure to complete basic training.

On the first hole I managed to get on the green in regulation. After hitting my birdie putt about a foot and a half past the hole, I marked my ball. Hogan knocked his putt to the lip and tapped in. The gallery ran toward the second tee. A thought suddenly occurred to me: these people weren't going to wait for me.

"Ken, that's going to happen all day long," Hogan said as we approached the second tee. "If you're not in my line, you go ahead and putt out, and then I'll putt."

"Thank you, Mr. Hogan," I said.

"Call me Ben," he said.

Call me Ben? I flashed back to when DiMaggio told me to call him Joe and Nelson told me to call him Byron. Now Hogan was telling me to call him Ben. I was on a first-name basis with my heroes! Of course, I didn't waste time abusing my new privilege. I must have called him Ben 10 times in the next two holes. "What a nice day, Ben." "Great shot, Ben." Ben this, Ben that. When we arrived at the 4th hole I teed off first, sending a 3 iron to within about six feet. He then hit *his* 3 iron right on line but into the front bunker. Walking toward the green, I still had the 3 iron in my hand. Without looking at me Hogan said, "Let me see that club."

"Excuse me, Ben," I said.

"I said let me see that club," he repeated.

I handed it over.

After taking a long look, he said, "You've got a bag of 1 irons, but it serves me right for looking into an amateur's bag." My 3 iron had less loft than his 3 iron.

Instantly I realized I had to take a stand. I couldn't let Hogan get away with a zinger like that, even if he was Ben Hogan.

"That's pretty good," I responded. "That's pretty good."

"What's pretty good?" Hogan said.

"I make a friend on the 2nd hole and I lose him on the 4th," I said. "I'm in the army, making 72 bucks a month. These are the only clubs I have. You want me to call you Mr. Hogan again?"

The strategy worked. Hogan appreciated it when people came back at him. I'm sure he was thinking: "This guy's got some balls." Too many people didn't come back at him. They were afraid. I wasn't; I was too young to be afraid of anyone.

"No," he said. "Call me Ben. But I want your address when we get in and I'm going to send you a decent set of clubs." He kept his word, sending me a brand-new set of Ben Hogan irons.

Our first round together in 1954 set the tone for our relationship. I considered myself incredibly lucky. Hogan, after all, didn't warm up to everyone. He was too consumed with his game for meaningless small talk, and he knew that I was the same way. We used to hold conversations with no words. A simple nod or a wink would say more than enough.

I made a respectable showing that week, tying for 16th with Jay Hebert, Peter Thomson, and Julius Boros, which earned me an automatic invitation to the 1955 Masters. I finished only eight shots behind Hogan and Snead, who met in an 18-hole playoff that Snead won, 70 to 71. Hogan had committed one of his rare mental errors during the 1954 Masters. In the 15th fairway, after hearing a loud roar, he assumed that Billy Joe Patton, the beloved amateur from North Carolina had knocked it on in two at the par-5 13th. So Hogan went for the green, not realizing that Patton had, actually, made a seven. The roar was a result of Patton choosing to go for it with a driver. Hogan never forgave himself for the lapse in judgment. "My fault," he said, "for not playing my own game."

Finishing as the third low amateur, I had proven that I could compete on one of the game's grand stages. I looked forward to when I would receive another opportunity.

It would be quite a while. The end of The Masters meant the end of my leave. I had no reason to complain because I had it pretty good, for being in the army. At least, I thought I did. When I returned to Fort Ord, I was placed in a new platoon with a different captain, who, for some reason, didn't like me and wasn't pleased with the leave I had been given. He changed my orders and sent me to another eight weeks of basic training. Before I knew it I was getting my head shaved again. I thought about lodging a formal protest with the general, but I sensed it would only make things worse. The captain had friends in high positions.

I set out immediately to make the best of the situation and I succeeded. One day I was invited to play nearby Del Monte Country Club. There was only one condition: I couldn't tell a soul. My company had the day off but was confined to the base. A captain in another platoon had arranged the game. I took full advantage, shooting a 63. Normally I would have turned my card in, but I couldn't. I kept it until after I was discharged.

During my off-duty hours, I helped to lay out Fort Ord's first golf course, the Bayonet Course. I even had my own room in the pro shop. What a deal, huh? I couldn't have fared much better in the civilian world. I was fortunate that Major General McClure, a participant in the Crosby Pro-Am and member of Cypress Point, believed you should do in the service what you did on the outside—which made me believe in him. Not even the captain out to nail me could mess this up.

But the United States Congress could. In 1954 Congress held hearings to investigate charges that the army was offering some of us preferential treatment, or "coddling athletes," as it was more commonly phrased. Football star Ollie Matson, the New York Yankees' Billy Martin, and myself were among the first brought forward to explain how we felt about being in the army. General McClure was being criticized in some quarters for giving me the leave to play in The Masters. The move was, reportedly, against official army policy. McClure, close to retirement, said he did it partly as a favor to Bobby Jones, who wanted me to participate, and also because it would show people that prominent sports figures were doing their duty for the country.

I handled the questions without trouble, mentioning how honored I was to serve. Matson also said the right things. We seemed to be in the clear until Martin spoke. I would find it hard to ever forgive what he said.

"I went to KP," Martin said, referring to kitchen duties such as washing dishes, peeling potatoes, and scrubbing pots. "These guys didn't have to do anything."

Martin was way out of line. We all went through KP. He also had no idea I went through 15 weeks of basic training and that I only worked on the golf course during my free time. No matter. Because of what Martin charged, new orders were cut for me, and they weren't good—I was headed to Korea. The war had been officially over for months, but we were still an occupying force. There were surely safer places to be, such as Denver, Colorado, where Martin was stationed. Talk about a coddled athlete! (Years later I ran into Martin when I was with New York Yankees' owner George Steinbrenner. "Do you remember Billy Martin?" Steinbrenner asked. Did I ever? "Were things tough in Colorado?" I said. Martin did not respond.)

Right before heading to Korea, my orders were changed again. This time, thank goodness, for the better. I would be going to Austria instead. I wasn't thrilled about leaving the United States, but Austria sure beat Korea. I'd be taking off in July.

First, there were a few things to take care of before I left . . . like getting married. Conni and I had discussed the subject, but I was planning to wait a year or so until I was discharged. When I received my orders, Conni insisted that we shouldn't wait. I wasn't too sure, but in those days, I pretty much went along with whatever she said. Looking back, I should have known we were making a mistake, but I was 23 years old, and everything was happening so fast. Conni must have sensed my ambivalence and realized that she'd better pin me down before it was too late.

Even though I was Catholic, we were married at a Presbyterian Church in Napa and went to Lake Tahoe for a brief honeymoon. I was on a week's leave. One would assume that I could offer tons of details about the wedding or the honeymoon, but I can't. I've always had a knack for being able to block out unpleasant memories, and getting married in 1954 is one instance where I've succeeded brilliantly. Was I in love with Conni? I suppose so, at least at one time. She was a beautiful woman. But I really knew nothing about love back then, about real commitment. Many years would pass before I would learn.

In Austria, Conni and I lived together for a few months in a small apartment away from the base. She was able to join me only because I had been promoted to infantry sergeant. The bedroom, kitchen, and living room were all one room. Such tight quarters could bring young newlyweds together, but in my case, it only amplified the growing doubts I was having about our relationship. I kept those doubts to myself. I was reserved, for one thing, and this was the fifties.

I focused instead on my responsibilities as a member of the infantry. My job was to help patrol the border in Linz, Austria, near the Iron Curtain. I never got into any actual combat, but I did receive a couple of good scares. One day, I shared a foxhole with another soldier who dropped a grenade. Panicking, he stared at it for what seemed to be an eternity. We didn't have an eternity. I fell to the ground, scooped it up, and threw the grenade as far as I could. Two more seconds, and they would have been our last two seconds. Another time, I heard an explosion. Before I knew what had happened, a piece of shrapnel hit me in my chest. To this day, I have no idea where it came from. I have a scar as a souvenir.

My only experience with death took place when we stopped at a nearby farmhouse while on patrol. We opened the door and the smell was horrific. There were five dead people inside. We never found out the whole story. (Many years later I walked into an apartment building in Hartford, Connecticut, and immediately realized that there was a dead body in the building. "How do you know?" others asked. "I will never forget that smell," I said.)

Unlike many veterans, I didn't collect a group of war buddies. I've never gone to reunions. At Christmas dinner in December 1954, I did meet up with Tommy Jacobs, a friend since our junior golf days in the Bay Area. Jacobs and I talked about our plans for life after the service. We never could have imagined that those plans would include a duel, 10 years later, for a U.S. Open title.

When the other soldiers headed straight for the bars during their off-duty hours—you could purchase a tall glass of beer for one mark, or 25 cents—I headed straight for the golf course. There was a 2,500-yard, par-31, nine-hole layout right next to our barracks. The course was no Augusta National, but I was not exactly in a position to be choosy. Borrowing a set of clubs, I got in some solid practice sessions. I once shot a 25, which I assumed was the course record. (This was one time, forgive me Byron, when I didn't ask who owned it.)

After being transferred from the infantry to special services, I was given a leave to play in a few tournaments. Though rusty, I did extremely well, winning the German Amateur and the Austrian Amateur. Granted, I wasn't playing the likes of Ben Hogan or Sam Snead, but a win was a win. Thousands of miles from home, taken away from my routine, I feared my game might never be the same.

My most challenging test came in the 1955 British Amateur at Royal Lytham & St. Annes, where I went up against Billy Joe Patton, the amateur who came so close to winning the 1954 Masters. Patton had me 1 down going to the 18th hole. After he secured his par, I lined up a 15-foot birdie putt to square the match. As I looked it over, Patton did the most bizarre thing. He walked to the back of the green and laid down. I was thinking, "What the heck is this guy doing?" Another thought then occurred to me: "What if I turned around and putted right into him?" He would automatically lose the hole for interfering with my ball. Ultimately, I couldn't do it. I couldn't win that way.

I didn't allow anything to interfere with my golf, not even Mother Nature. I practiced my swing in combat boots and fatigues and painted the balls red and green to spot them in the snow. A little over the top? Maybe so, but working on the game I loved is what preserved my sanity over there, especially when things didn't get any better between Conni and me. In the summer of 1955 Conni went back to California. No, we weren't planning for a divorce. We were making plans, believe it or not, for a new family. I suppose we did what a lot of people did in the fifties: hoped a baby might solve our problems. The baby was due in March. Over the next few months Conni and I hardly wrote to each other, another sign we chose to ignore.

In October I headed home, at last, though I almost didn't make it. On the flight from Rome to Tripoli, the plane lost two engines. I was handed a parachute. I survived all this time overseas, I thought, only to die in the middle of the Mediterranean. I can't describe how relieved I was when we landed safely in Tripoli.

Looking back, I can say without hesitation that I hated the army. I can also say I wouldn't trade the experience for anything. I learned discipline, direction, and duty. I'm 100 percent American, which is why I was furious with Muhammad Ali for dodging the draft during the Vietnam War. I considered his act of defiance an attack on America. I met him once in Chicago, posing for a group picture during an awards ceremony. I would not pose for a picture with only the two of us. I thought about all the kids who had sacrificed their lives while he hid behind his religion.

Chapter Five

BACK IN THE U.S.A.

I can't overemphasize how gratified I felt to be home again after 16 months overseas. I didn't care if I never left America again. I look at today's golfers who achieve so much at such a young age, and I come to a simple conclusion: there is no draft. The only academies they attend specialize in golf. Before these youngsters reach puberty, they develop their careers without fear that, depending on world events, the whole plan could change in an instant.

Once I gained my bearings, I set out to make a living. Besides myself and Conni, there would soon be another mouth to feed, and there was no sense wasting any time. Fortunately, there was a position waiting for me at Lowery's dealership. I spent some time at Lake Merced Motors in the service department to learn the business from the ground up. I was soon switched to sales, and before long I had my pitch down flat.

"Here is my bottom line [price varied depending on the vehicle]," I'd say. "I'm not going to sit here and fool around because

I've got to eat lunch at 12:00 and I tee off at 1:00. So if you can beat that price, I'll buy one, too, because I can sell it and make a profit."

The buyer would often come back the next day, with the usual response:

"I'll take the car," he'd say. "I can't beat it."

I was a good salesman. Within 90 days, on a staff of 24, I took third place in most cars sold. One morning, an unshaven fellow with cowboy boots wandered into the showroom. One of the other salesmen, a real smart-ass, immediately assumed the cowboy was not going to make him a sizable commission.

"You're trying to learn the business," the salesman told me. "You take that guy. I don't want him. I'm going to lunch."

The cowboy was mine. That's what happens when you're the new guy. I introduced myself, and within moments, the cowboy got down to business.

"I'll tell you what you do," he said, admiring the Mark II Coupes in the showroom. "You give me a price. I'd like the powder blue one for my wife and the gray one for myself."

I gave him my best price, which he accepted without any attempt to negotiate. I took his check and told him I would be right back. "That's right, son," he said. "I don't blame you at all. You go ahead and make sure that my check is good."

His check was good, all right. The bank told me that this unshaven cowboy was loaded; he could afford to buy the whole agency. The story got around the office pretty fast, angering the salesman when he returned from lunch. He demanded half of the commission, and when I refused, he went to Lowery. I didn't care. I knew I did the right thing. So did Lowery, who fired the guy on the spot. I eventually became the vice president of that dealership.

The moral of the story? The most difficult challenge, I suppose, can often lead to the most satisfying reward. I would discover this over and over in golf *and* in life.

I made good money working for Lowery, about $30,000 in salary and commission. No wonder the thought of turning pro never occurred to me. In 1955, for instance, Julius Boros, the leading money winner on the tour, earned only about $63,000. Factoring in all the expenses—hotels, meals, transportation—crisscrossing the country to play golf was a brutal way to make a living. I wonder about the outstanding players who never tried. What might they have been able to achieve?

The job provided something as valuable as money—freedom. When I wasn't selling cars, I was playing golf. My game, to be fair, required some serious work after I returned from Austria. Practicing in combat boots in the snow was not such a smart idea, after all. I developed a number of very poor habits. Lowery couldn't believe how much my swing had deteriorated. He immediately placed an emergency call to Byron Nelson.

"You have to get over here," he told Nelson. "He's in bad shape."

Nelson met us in Palm Springs, shortly after the 1955 Ryder Cup matches were staged at Thunderbird Country Club. When he first started to observe me, I thought he was going to pass out. But a week later, thanks to his patience, I was back to normal.

The big money games were Tuesdays at California Golf Club and Fridays at San Francisco Golf Club. Lowery no longer had to cover me. Harvie Ward, who was also selling cars for Lowery, and I cleaned up. We were, as a matter of fact, too good. One day, we won a few bucks from some guy—Ward shot 63 and I shot 64. The guy would never play us again.

In January of 1956 Ward and I teamed up for a match at Cypress Point against opponents who were a little tougher. The match would go down as one of the classics.

Ward and I were in the Monterey Peninsula to compete in the Crosby. During a cocktail party before the tournament, George Coleman, a big oilman from Oklahoma, along with Bing Crosby, Eddie Lowery, and Paul Shields, another prominent businessman, were casually asking us what our plans were for the following day. We didn't really have any, we told them. I can't recall exactly how the idea popped into my mind, but I blurted out: "Harvie and I would like to play Byron and Ben." Nelson and Hogan were also preparing for the Crosby; Hogan was to team up with Bing and Nelson with Lowery. Coleman didn't waste a moment. He knew a great idea when he heard one.

"The two kids want to play you and Byron," Coleman told Hogan.

"I'd play," Hogan responded, "but I don't think Byron would play."

Lowery then found Nelson. He was determined to make this work.

"The two kids wants to play you and Hogan," he said.

"I'd play," Nelson said, "but I don't think Ben would play."

Just like that, the match was on. Hogan, as usual, took the lead. "Make me a starting time tomorrow for 11:00 A.M. at Pebble Beach," he said.

"Ben," I said. "What do you mean? We're not playing Pebble. We're playing Cypress Point at 10:00."

"I know that," he said, "but I don't want people coming over there and watching me play against a couple of *amateurs*." He gave me one of his familiar winks. I looked at him and started to laugh. We both had a big grin.

The next morning couldn't come quickly enough. I was going to play against my two heroes, both of whom had influenced me in more ways than I could ever describe. The most amazing thing was that they were no longer just heroes. They were friends. Besides, getting Nelson and Hogan to play on the same team was next to impossible. I don't recall the two of them ever playing a practice round or having dinner. While they shared tremendous respect for each other, they were not particularly close. Except for golf, I suppose, they had very little in common. On top of everything else, the match was set for Cypress Point, my favorite course.

Once we arrived on the first tee, I stopped thinking of them as heroes or friends. They were opponents. I wanted to win as badly as ever and was confident that Ward and I could take them. Amateurs or not, we had plenty of game, and, as usual, there was some money on the line. The four of us played for a $100 Nassau, which was a lot of money in those days. Coleman, Lowery, Shields, and a few members of Cypress Point put up more dough.

They could afford it.

The match was close the whole way, with no side ever seizing more than a one-hole advantage. After nine, we were all square.

At the par-5 10th, Hogan was short of the green in two. He then pitched in from about 40 yards for three to put his team 1 up. The next three holes were halved. The 14th was halved in pars, only the third time all day nobody registered a birdie. At the magnificent, often overshadowed, short par-3 15th hole, after Nelson and Ward made par, Hogan made a 12-foot putt for a two. I matched him from 10 feet. Nelson and Ward both birdied the famous 16th and 17th, leaving us still 1 down with one hole to go.

By this time, the match was no longer our precious little secret. With word quickly spreading across the peninsula, we drew the spectators we had hoped to avoid. In retrospect, I'm glad they showed up. They saw the kind of golf they were likely to never see again.

At 18, I hit my approach to within about 12 feet. Hogan hit next to about 10 feet. I made my putt, setting the stage for Hogan. Part of me, strangely enough, was rooting for Hogan to make the putt. Why? Well, because he was Ben Hogan, I suppose, and he wasn't going to be around forever.

"OK, Ben, knock it in," Nelson said. "We can win."

Hogan didn't need any encouragement.

"I'm not about to be tied by a couple of amateurs," he said, giving me another wink.

The putt was dead center the whole way. Who, after all, would expect anything different from Ben Hogan?

We all shook hands, went into the locker room, put on our coats and ties, and then entered the clubhouse. Everyone felt proud. Among the four of us, there were 27 birdies and an eagle. Ward and Nelson shot 67s, I finished with a 65, and Hogan recorded a 63. Nearly 50 years later, I am asked about that round constantly.

"I'll tell you one thing," Hogan said in the clubhouse. "I didn't want you to know it, but we wanted to beat you guys so bad. I told Byron, 'We've got our hands full with these guys,' and Byron said, 'You can bet on that.' That's as hard as I can ever remember playing but that was some fun. I didn't want the round to end."

"If there was one more hole," I said, "we would have gotten you."

A few days later, the Crosby started. Funny, isn't it? I can remember almost every hole of the match with Hogan and Nelson, but the actual tournament is a total blur. I've played many tournaments in my lifetime, but I played against Hogan and Nelson only once.

Next up was a tournament that could never be a blur—the City Championship. I was the defending champion—well, sort of. I won the last time I was entered, in 1953 against Art Linhares, but I missed the following two years because of the army. I was anxious to make up for it.

I was not the favorite. Harvie Ward was, and with good reason. Ward, the winner in 1955, was also the reigning U.S. Amateur champion and one of the most successful amateurs in the game. Could Ward have been an outstanding pro, perhaps even a major championship winner? There is no doubt, if he had been willing to apply himself. Ward drove the ball straight as an arrow and was an excellent putter, but he didn't spend countless hours on the range. In 1957, he lost his amateur status for a year by accepting gifts from his sponsor. Frankly, and it's not because he's a close friend, I have always believed the punishment was too severe. What he did was nothing compared to what amateurs get away with today.

I was motivated, but I was also distracted. Conni and I, occupying a two-bedroom ranch house in the middle-class suburb of Westlake, were expecting our child in mid-March, right around the time the final match would be played. I might have had doubts about marriage, but I had no doubts about being a father, probably because my own father was such a good role model.

As Ward and I, in opposite sides of the draw, eliminated one opponent after another at Harding Park, the hype began to build. We became the talk of the dealership and the city. Everybody wanted to witness a dream matchup. Finally, on March 11, everybody got what they wanted. The turnout was estimated at about twelve thousand people, the largest gallery for a City Final since the tournament's inception in 1917. The atmosphere felt like a major. It *was* a major.

Arriving at the first tee, I made an opening statement.

"Harvie, you took the city away from me while I was gone," I said. "I'm going to get it back. You are the defending champion, and we're the best of friends, but I'm going to whip your ass like I've never whipped anybody's ass before."

Ward did not flinch. He smiled. "Good, I'm going to get you, too," he said. "So let's go out and have some fun."

I certainly did, making a birdie at the first hole to go 1 up. At the par-5 10th, I made an even louder statement. My second shot ended up to the right by the trees, leaving me with a nearly impossible approach over the bunker. I knocked down a 4 iron, running it through the bunker to within five feet of the cup. Knowing it was a miraculous shot, I quickly looked at Ward.

"I don't think I'm going to win," he said.

"I'm glad you got the message," I told him.

I led by 3 after the morning round. Ward narrowed the deficit to 2 at the 24th hole, but I came back the very next hole. I wouldn't let him gain any momentum. Finally, at the 32nd, I clinched the match, winning 5 and 4. For the third time in seven years, the City was mine.

After some celebrating, I went home. I slept only a few hours before Conni woke me up. There was about to be something else to celebrate.

We packed our belongings for the trip to the hospital. Just then, Ward called to check up on Conni. After I gave him the update, he said he would meet us there. For four hours, as I paced anxiously in the waiting room, Ward stayed with me every minute, being the best friend a man could ever have. Only a few hours earlier, we were trying to beat each other's brains out on the golf course. Now, on the same side, we were finding out what was truly important.

We went over the match, shot after shot, as the time went by.

"I knew I was dead after I saw that shot at 10," Ward said.

Finally the doctor came out. "You have a son," he said.

The news didn't fully register at first. I was so consumed with making sure the baby was healthy. Then, it dawned on me: a son. I had a son. We named him Matthew Bruce. He weighed seven pounds and 13 ounces. Byron and Louise Nelson became his godparents.

We were a family. Conni and I still had our problems, but with Matthew, we hoped perhaps the atmosphere might improve. In any case, I didn't believe in giving up, on the course or at home. As my dad always told me: "Giving up is the only thing that takes no talent."

First things first. A week or so after Matt and Conni came home, I left. I headed back to Augusta National, at last. My tie for 16th in 1954 had qualified me for the 1955 Masters, but the commute from Austria was a bit too far. While I was taking orders from a major, Hogan, Demaret, Snead, and company were trying to win one. Believe me, this didn't escape my attention, although I was really hurting in June of 1955 when the U.S. Open was staged at the Olympic Club. If I had qualified, I would have been greeted as the local kid who made good, and knowing the golf course as well as I did, I might have made a run at the championship. But while Jack Fleck pulled off his amazing upset of Ben Hogan, all I could do was follow the action in the *Stars and Stripes*.

I was very grateful to Hogan, Nelson, Demaret, and the other nine former Masters champions. Appreciating the fact that I had served my country, they voted to give me an invitation.

I wasn't about to waste my opportunity. To prepare, I entered the Phoenix Open, finishing a very respectable sixth. My confidence was higher than ever.

Chapter Six

A LOSS LIKE NO OTHER

Driving down Magnolia Lane in April of 1956 was just as magical as it had been two years earlier. There is nothing quite like that feeling in all of golf, maybe all of sports. With only a few exceptions—1964, two years in the seventies, and the 2003 tournament, when I purposely kept my distance from Lanny Wadkins, my replacement in the 18th tower—I've been back to Augusta every year since. I experience the same chills each time. However, being there in 1956 felt different than it had in 1954. I wasn't a naïve 22-year-old anymore. I was an army veteran, a husband, a father, and a serious contender for the championship.

If I was optimistic, it was nothing compared to Eddie Lowery. He put down $5,000 on me to win, $5,000 to place, and $5,000 to show, getting excellent odds—12-1, 10-1, and 8-1. Fortunately, just like my match with Martin Stanovich in the 1950 City Championship, I didn't know there was any action on me. I could have cracked.

My confidence soared even higher during practice rounds with Byron Nelson. I felt as if we were back on our exhibition tour. Watching him, I realized once again the value of golf management, of knowing where to hit it, and, more important, where to miss it. At Augusta National, landing on the wrong side of the hole usually results in the loss of one, maybe two shots. Nelson, though retired and living on his farm in Roanoke, Texas, remained a supreme strategist. And I remained a very attentive student.

I was also feeling comfortable away from the course, which always makes a huge difference during tournament week. Ward and I stayed at a rented house with Lowery.

Enough of the preliminaries. Let's play!

"On the tee, Ken Venturi."

I always love the way they announce introductions at The Masters. With no reference to previous titles or honors, every player is reminded that he starts with a clean slate, with the past as irrelevant as the future. Only the present matters. I was ready. Moments before teeing off, I caught a quick glance at the leader board. All the big-name players were prominently displayed: Ben Hogan, Sam Snead, Byron Nelson, Cary Middlecoff, and a handful of others.

"Your name is not there," said Margaret Lowery, Eddie's wife.

"Just give me a few holes," I assured her. "I'll get it up there."

Which is exactly what I did. Playing in a drizzle, I birdied the first hole from 20 feet, the second from about 5, and the third from 12. I made it four in a row with a beautiful 4 iron approach to within a foot. My name was soon on leader boards all over the course. Even I didn't imagine it was going to happen that fast. I couldn't birdie every hole, though I tried. I was in one of those zones. Besides, at the age of 24, playing for nothing but pride, I could fire away without fear.

I parred the rest of the front nine for a 4-under 32, and escaped with pars on 10, 11, and 12, the toughest three-hole stretch on the course. I arrived at 13, the hole that many, including myself, considered the premier par-5 in the game. Rae's Creek crosses in front of the green and runs along the left side of the fairway. It's a hole that players can reach in two, but on which they can also get high scores. That's why it was considered a great risk/reward par-5. The idea was to draw it off the tee so you would be able to reach the green in two. Go too far left on your drive and you go into the woods; too far right, and you've got no angle to the green. In the years ahead, I would spend countless hours at 13 for CBS, watching dreams of Masters glory—Curtis Strange, David Duval, Vijay Singh, and Ernie Els spring to mind—perish in Rae's Creek. No other hole in golf offered so much promise and so much pain.

My drive didn't go as far as I would have liked, presenting me with the familiar choice: to go or not to go. I went. What did I have to lose? I nailed my trusty 3 wood, sailing past the creek easily, and faced a tough, uphill 20-footer for eagle. My playing partner, Billy Joe Patton, putted first from about 30 feet away for his eagle. When the ball dropped the crowd went nuts. They adored Patton, probably because he was from the South. He, too, went nuts, dancing around the green, waving his putter in the air. Hey, I was all for a player showing emotion, but Patton was starting to get carried away.

"Get your ball out of the hole," I said, finally. "You're only going to get a halve." He smiled, and I laughed, as well.

After he stepped aside, I made my eagle, just as I predicted. Now it was my turn to go nuts—inside, of course; I wasn't the demonstrative type. Walking off the green, Patton shook my hand and congratulated me, and I congratulated him.

I parred the 14th, which would later be my Masters nemesis, and finished with a 6-under 66, the lowest score ever by an amateur in The Masters. Reaching 16 greens in regulation, with eight one-putt greens, I was one stroke ahead of Middlecoff, the defending champion. Tommy Bolt and Shelley Mayfield were two back, Hogan three behind. To say I was pumped up would be a colossal understatement. There was no reason for me to believe I couldn't win.

The only drawback to the 66 was that I had to meet with the reporters. I was prepared for the course; I wasn't prepared for them. In California, even when I performed well, there were never more than a few members of the Fourth Estate around at any time. To me, the group at Augusta looked like a convention. What would I say? What would they write?

I decided, as usual, to keep my answers relatively brief. The less I said, the less chance there was that they would find out about my stammering. Of course, by being so cautious, I risked another problem: they might think I was cocky. There was little I could do, and I did better than I anticipated. The stories made me a hero—for a day, at least.

In the second round I was paired with Jimmy Demaret, who won The Masters in 1940, 1947, and 1950. (I still can't understand why Augusta National has failed to acknowledge such a deserving champion, not even with a plaque. The only explanation I can think of is that he and Cliff Roberts, the former tournament chairman, didn't see eye to eye.) Demaret, who would become one of my dearest friends, was the ideal playing partner, helping me to keep my feet on the ground. We were only in the second round. There was, as the saying goes, a lot of golf left to be played.

For me it was a lot of good golf. I fired a 2-under 34 on the front, highlighted by an eagle at the par-5 8th. After two shots, I was about 125 feet from the hole. I took out my 6 iron and bumped the ball to the top of a ridge. It ran down right into the cup. More important, I was on my way perhaps to another 66.

Slow down, Venturi, I tried to tell myself, but it was apparently too late. I bogeyed 11 and 12 and was suddenly in danger of posting a round closer to 76. The wind dried out the greens, forcing players to aim away from the flags. I had to stop the bleeding, and fast.

Fortunately I did. I birdied the two holes you absolutely have to birdie on the back nine—13 and 15—and picked up another important stroke at 18. The 69 was again the lowest round of the day, giving me a two-day total of 135, tying the 36-hole mark set by Henry Picard (1935) and Byron Nelson (1942). I enjoyed a four-stroke lead over Middlecoff. Two rounds, two to go. If this was a dream, well, I didn't want to ever wake up.

Augusta National cared little about my dream, or, for that matter, anyone else's dreams. On Saturday the course decided to fight back. The winds picked up and dried out the greens even more. The day's mission was to survive. Through nine holes, I failed. I shot a miserable 40, missing a slew of makeable putts, including a two-footer at the ninth. Just like that, my lead had evaporated. Middlecoff, playing in the third group behind me, recorded a 35 on the front. I dropped another shot at the 11th. There was no reason to think that I could turn it around.

Somehow I did, with consecutive birdies at 13, 14, and 15. At 13 and 15, I played it safe both times, laying up short of the hazard. This was not the time to be a hero. I couldn't win the tournament on Saturday, but I sure could lose it. Sandwiched between those two holes was a magnificent approach at 14 that nearly went in for an eagle. All in all, I finished with a 3-over 75, which sounds pretty horrific until it's stacked up against the other scores that day: Jackie Burke (75), Bolt (78), Doug Ford (75), and

Middlecoff (75). The biggest blunder came from Middlecoff, who needed only a par at 18 to close within two shots. But he 3-putted from five feet for a double bogey. Bottom line: I ended the third round exactly where I started it, four shots ahead of the field. There was only one round to go.

After I met with the press again, Cliff Roberts and Bobby Jones said they had to see me. There was a "problem."

Problem? Did I commit a rules violation? Did I make an inappropriate comment? No, it was neither of those things. The problem was that, according to Masters tradition, the third-round leader was paired on the final day with Byron Nelson. But Roberts and Jones felt that, in this case, that wouldn't be such a hot idea. "We feel, Ken, that you're going to win," Jones said, "but we don't want people to say that Byron tutored you, that he clubbed you and talked to you as he was taking you around. We don't want anything to interfere with your great victory."

I understood. Nothing would please Jones more than to see an amateur win the tournament that he built from scratch. He was an amateur his whole life. That's why, if it were to happen, I had to win the right way.

Jones and Roberts put the ball in my court. I could pick any other player in the field to be my partner. There were numerous options: Mike Souchak, Jackie Burke, Jimmy Demaret, Ben Hogan, Tommy Bolt. I opted not to select any of them. I went instead with Slammin' Sammy Snead.

Why Snead? After all, I barely knew the guy. The final round of The Masters sure seemed like a strange time to get acquainted.

There was a method, I insist, to my madness. I was tutored by the great Nelson and played practice rounds with the great

Hogan. Now I was going to win The Masters walking side by side with the great Snead, the third member of the magical triumvirate. And, make no mistake about it, I was going to win. I was going to wear a green jacket. Jones and Roberts agreed. They said, "*when* you win," not "*if* you win."

I went back to the house and slept like a baby. There was no reason to be concerned. All I had to do was the same thing I had been doing all week long.

I was just as confident on the driving range the next morning. My swing looked good. Even the prospect of another tough, windy day didn't deter me. Everybody would deal with the same conditions.

But on my way to the clubhouse, only minutes from my tee time, it happened.

"How does it feel," the stranger asked, "to be the first amateur to win The Masters? You know you'll make millions."

I brushed the guy off, but the damage had been done. He was right. I was going to win The Masters, which was being shown, for the first time, on national television. The victory would change my life. I would become the most celebrated amateur since Jones. I started to get tears in my eyes. With the business offers that were sure to come my way, I would be able to buy my parents new cars or a new house. I suddenly started to think about all the possibilities, when thinking about anything except my game was the last thing I should be doing on the final day of a major championship.

I promptly 3-putted the first hole. I parred the second, however, and managed to hang in there, only 1 over for the day heading to the ninth. I wasn't the same player from the first three rounds, but, even after another 3-putt bogey at 9, giving me a 38 on the front, I was now leading by five shots. Middlecoff, my closest pursuer at the start of the day, wasn't making any kind of a move. The only player doing anything substantial was Burke, but he had started the day eight shots behind.

Nobody wins The Masters coming from eight shots behind.

At the turn, I made another huge mental error.

"I got this wrapped up," I said to myself. "If I can shoot 38, I win this tournament." Thirty-eight? I hadn't been thinking 38 the whole week, my whole life! That kind of attitude made me too conservative, just the opposite of how I played the first 63 holes.

I proceeded to bogey 10, 11, and 12. My lead, as well as my sanity, was slipping away even further. It is difficult even today, almost 50 years later, to describe what it felt like, and what little there was I could do about it. All I can say is that it's the most horrible feeling in the world. I'm sure Greg Norman knows what I mean.

After a par on 13, the feeling grew even worse with 3-putt bogeys at 14 and 15. I nearly 4-putted 14, making a three-footer for bogey. Yet, as I approached the 17th tee, all was not lost. Middlecoff was still struggling. I then found out what Burke was doing, and that I would need two pars to force an 18-hole play-off. I was shocked, to say the least. At 17, after a perfect drive, I pulled out my 8 iron to aim at a pin tucked behind the bunker.

Forget about par, I thought. I could make birdie, par the 18th, and win this thing outright.

I hit a good shot, but at that precise moment, a gust of wind came up, sending the ball over the green. I chipped to within six feet but missed the putt. Burke, meanwhile, got his par on 18, finishing with a 71. Suddenly, incredibly, I was trailing by one.

At 18, I hit my second shot to within about 20 feet. The putt at first looked good, but then moved sharply to the left. It suddenly hit me. I wasn't going to be able to buy my parents a new car or a new house. I wasn't going to win The Masters after all. I shot an 80.

I know it sounds absurd, but I didn't really play that poorly. I reached 15 greens in regulation. What killed me were six 3-putts, while Burke didn't register one the whole tournament. I kept hitting the ball to the wrong side of the hole. Did I choke? Well, I suppose, if you go by my score, you can make that argument. I choose to look at it differently. The day was tough for everyone. In fact, Burke and Snead were the only two players to break par.

As horrible as I felt, I remembered what my mother told me: "Don't ever cry in defeat." I maintained my composure throughout the traditional green jacket ceremony. I said all the proper things, even earning praise from Roberts and Jones for the way I handled such a devastating setback. What else could I do? I knew I would be remembered for losing the tournament. I didn't also want to be remembered for losing my cool.

The flight back to San Francisco was the longest of my life. I replayed much of the final round in my head, and it wouldn't be the last time. Over the following weeks, months, and years, that round would come back to me in the middle of the night, and the result was always the same. I don't wish that kind of nightmare on anyone.

By the time the plane touched down in San Francisco, I was still feeling pretty low. At least I would be surrounded by sympathetic faces, and believe me, I needed all the support I could get. Unfortunately, as I made my way inside the terminal, I was surrounded by other faces that weren't quite sympathetic. They were members of the press. They came to welcome me home, but they also came for a story.

No problem. I knew how the game was played. Or, at least, I thought I knew. What took place over the next half hour or so would damage my reputation for years. I would have a hard time trusting the press again. I would always make myself available, but there were so many things I wouldn't tell them.

The group, which included several writers I knew fairly well, asked how I got along with Snead and how I felt about the change in pairings for the final round.

I got along with Snead just fine, I told them. He tried to talk to me, but because I was so nervous, he pretty much left me alone.

In reference to the pairings, I explained what Jones and Roberts told me, that they didn't want it to be "a hollow victory."

Finally, in an attempt to comfort my mother, who was crying her eyes out—she could cry in defeat—I said, "Don't worry, Mom. We'll show 'em. We'll win the Open."

There were no more questions. I did well. That wasn't so bad, I figured, as far as these things go. I figured wrong.

The next day, the headlines said it all:

"Sam Snead gave Venturi the silent treatment."

"Venturi says they didn't want an amateur to win so they changed the pairings."

"Venturi vows to get revenge. Says he'll win the Open."

The story also mentioned that I accused Mike Souchak of helping Burke choose clubs and read the greens, and that The Masters officials shouldn't have kept Harvie Ward, who was in the gallery, from conversing with me over the final holes.

I was incensed. The reporters had gotten the story all wrong, and now I was going to pay the price. I had tried to explain what happened, but the quotes were taken out of context. The account circulated throughout the country, making me come off like a sore, arrogant loser. The power of the pen had struck another victim. In a strange way, the only positive result of the whole episode was that it helped me overcome the actual loss much quicker. There wasn't enough room for both depression and anger.

Once I simmered down, the question remained: What do I do now? Nothing, I decided. Over time, this whole mess would blow over. There was no reason to make it worse than it already was. After all, I hadn't done anything wrong, and sooner or later people would come to the same conclusion.

Imagine my sense of outrage when, a few days later, I read in the papers about a 184-word telegram of apology I sent to Bobby Jones and Cliff Roberts. It read:

> *Deeply regret embarrassment to both of you and Augusta National Golf Club for impulsive statements to press upon return to San Francisco. I am sorry that I made them. I certainly believe rules of golf were not broken at Masters tournament. I was misunderstood on two statements. First that I would have won had I played with Byron Nelson and two that Mike Souchak clubbed and read the greens for Burke. I did not make these statements and have asked press to correct them. Was naturally disappointed that Byron Nelson was not my playing companion in final round after he was originally named, but now appreciate committee's reason for making change in pairing. My statements from the heart were made*

at ceremonies after the final round. I would appreciate having these stand. Namely quote I was disappointed at losing. Jackie Burke's victory was a wonderful achievement. The galleries and Augusta National members were very friendly to me and I hope to be back next year unquote. I have learned a valuable lesson. I wish to go on record as having no excuses for losing.

Was I hallucinating? These were not my words, nor were they words I had approved. They were the words of Eddie Lowery, who, without consulting me, sent a telegram in *my name* to Augusta National.

The telegram was Lowery's idea of damage control.

When I confronted him, he tried to defend the strategy.

"I felt it was the best thing to do under the circumstances," he told me. "And now we'll all get past this."

I couldn't have disagreed more. The telegram made me look guilty, and I was anything but guilty. Getting past "this" would be more difficult than ever. I remained friends with Eddie Lowery for the rest of his life—he died in 1984—but I never felt the same about him again.

Roberts and Jones responded publicly to my apology, calling it "a splendid and courageous effort . . . vindication of our confidence that his true sentiments had been expressed in the press conference after the tournament . . . and wish to assure him of the warmest kind of welcome upon his return to Augusta." They also said that "no one could have conducted himself more becomingly than Ken did in Augusta after a heartbreaking experience." Even with those kind words, I still felt then, and as I do now, that the apology was the wrong move.

To be fair, I received my share of support, with more than 100 telegrams pouring in. My favorite came from President Eisenhower, which read:

> *Dear Mr. Venturi, I want to tell you that I saw the entire one-hour televised coverage of The Masters during the last round. In many respects, it was an all-time thriller, and to my way of thinking, a great share of the credit for making it belongs to you. I know that most all of the Augusta National members want to see an amateur win a Masters championship. If you are next year the first pupil to defeat the teachers of the game, on this course, it will come as no surprise to me. This time I was one member who was openly pulling for you. So, without detracting from the fine performance of such a good player and sportsman as Jack Burke, here's luck to you next year. With best wishes, Dwight Eisenhower.*

I became friendly with President Eisenhower during the late fifties and early sixties. I was with him at Eldorado Country Club in Indian Wells, California, along with Freeman Gosden, star of the *Amos 'n' Andy* radio show, when Ike recorded one of the best rounds of his life. Ike made four birdies, twice as many as he ever posted in a single round. When we went inside for drinks, he went over the round, hole by hole, shot by shot. Finally, realizing I would be late for a dinner date with Beau—my second wife whom I was courting at the time—I said, as politely as I could manage, "Mr. President, I really have to go. Congratulations on those four birdies, that was really good." He answered: "Thank you, Ken. We'll play again. By the way, what did you shoot?" "Sixty-four," someone else told him. "That's a nice round, Ken," Eisenhower said, still focusing on his own achievements, "but I'll never forget my four birdies."

I lost more than a tournament on that April afternoon in 1956. I lost a future. There is little doubt that, if I had won, William Ford, chairman of the Ford Motor Company, would have made me one of his vice presidents (he told me so a year later). With all the shares of Ford stock that I would have received, money would never have been a problem again. I'm also certain that, to honor the title, I would have stayed an amateur forever, and would have been chosen by Jones, as he later told me, to succeed him at The Masters. All that was gone now.

Yet looking at the way my life turned out, the 80 was the best thing that ever happened to me. Otherwise, I never would have staged my comeback. I never would have met Beau. I never would have met Kathleen (my present wife). I never would have done television for 35 years.

I never would have become the man I am today.

At home in San Francisco with my mom and dad, Fred and Ethyl Venturi.

That's me as a teenager in the forties. I was a shy kid who grew to love the solitude I found on the golf course.

That's our 1953 Walker Cup team. I'm the fifth one from the right. From left are Charley Yates (captain), Jack Westland, Dick Chapman, Harvie Ward, Don Cherry, Sam Urzetta, myself, Gene Littler, James Jackson, Charlie Coe, and William Campbell. Photo courtesy of Norman Fortier.

Here Billy Joe Patton congratulates me after my opening-round 66 at the 1956 Masters, the lowest score ever by an amateur at The Masters. I don't have to tell you how that one ended up. Photo courtesy of Frank Christian Studios.

My dear friend and trusted mentor, the great Byron Nelson. I couldn't help but learn just from watching and being around him. Photo courtesy of Gayle Studios.

This birdie on 18 capped a wild rally on the back nine at Augusta to hold the lead after day two of the 1958 Masters. But I was still to suffer another agonizing loss on the final day. Photo courtesy of AP/Wide World Photos.

Masters miseries behind me, here I'm collecting a bonus check from U.S. Royal after winning the 1959 Los Angeles Open.

That's Father Francis Kevin Murray in the middle. He taught me as much about trust, confidence, and dedication—about my inner self—as Byron Nelson taught me about golf. On the left is Bud Binyon. Photo courtesy of Bill Mark.

At Pebble Beach for the start of Bob Hope's annual tournament. This all-star lineup included, from left, Harvie Ward, Doug Ford, myself, George Bayer, Bob Hope, Bing Crosby, Cary Middlecoff, and Mike Souchak.

After I won the '64 Open, press committee member Jimmy Johnson led me to the area where I could take calls from my parents and other well-wishers. Here I'm on the line with Bing Crosby, whom I learned was reduced to tears as he watched the final holes. Photo courtesy of Bill Mark.

Relaxing before a round with baseball greats Joe DiMaggio (left) and Lefty O'Doul. Photo courtesy of Bob Campbell.

Another baseball immortal, Willie Mays of my hometown San Francisco Giants, let me give him some pointers before a game in 1960.

Chapter Seven

ON THE ROAD

I went back to normal life in San Francisco—at least, as normal as possible. I sold more cars and played more golf. I tried to be the best husband to Conni and the best father to Matt. As always, I did whatever I could to make my parents proud. That wasn't going to change because I lost a golf tournament, even if it was The Masters. I had lost golf tournaments before, and I was going to lose them again.

Besides, I had to prepare for the next big tournament, the United States Open. The Open in 1956 was to be played at Oak Hill Country Club in Rochester, New York. As a teenager, when I did commentary alone on the range at Harding, I always fantasized about winning the Open, never The Masters. Maybe that's why I lost The Masters the way I did. Maybe it was all going to be a perfect setup for a magical triumph at the 1956 Open. Cue the music.

Some fantasy, all right. There would be no magic and no music, at least not in Rochester. I opened with a 77, putting me in danger of missing the cut. I didn't have to worry about a press conference this time. But, just when all seemed lost, I rebounded with rounds of 71, 68, and 73 to finish eighth, eight shots behind the winner, Cary Middlecoff. My 68 tied Bob Rosburg and Ben Hogan for the low round of the week. After my collapse at Augusta, I was extremely proud of how well I rebounded from such an abysmal start. Two top 10s in two majors wasn't too shabby.

My next major challenge would take place at the United States Amateur, to be staged at the Knollwood Club in Lake Forest, Illinois, just outside of Chicago. For some reason I had never done particularly well in the Amateur. My best finish was in 1953, when I lost to Arnold Palmer in the fourth round. This time, considering what I had accomplished in recent months—my third City Championship, a second-place finish in Augusta, and a top 10 in the U.S. Open—capturing the Amateur appeared attainable. What made it more enticing was the strong possibility of another duel in the final with Harvie Ward. Ward, in the opposite bracket again, was the defending champion. After what I had done to him in the City Final five months earlier, he would be out to get even. I welcomed the challenge.

After I won two matches, my third-round opponent was Bob Roos, a longtime friend from San Francisco. Getting by Roos would be a mere formality. When we played at home, I used to give him two strokes a side and still beat him pretty handily in a five-dollar Nassau. But, as I should have known, no match in golf is a mere formality. Roos birdied the 18th hole to win 1 up. I was an early loser in the Amateur yet again.

The loss itself was not too disconcerting, especially compared to the heartbreak of Augusta. But what it meant concerned me much more: my heart was no longer in amateur golf. There could be no other possible explanation for a loss to, of all people, Bob

Roos. Even the prospect of another battle with Ward failed to fire me up.

There was only one thing for me to do: turn professional. To be honest, the idea had been floating around in my mind for several months, ever since the Masters collapse. I felt like it might be the only way I could prove that I was not what everyone was saying about me. I was not a choker.

On the other hand, there was an even more compelling reason for why I *shouldn't* become a professional golfer: the almighty dollar. I would be turning down a secure job at the dealership to take my chances against the best players in the world. Even if I did reasonably well, I still wouldn't earn what I made working, between salary and commission, for Eddie Lowery. With a new child to feed, turning my back on a secure job was hardly the most prudent thing to do. The months dragged on and on as I kept weighing the pros and cons.

Then came the loss to Roos. Risky or not, I had to make my move. First I discussed the matter with Conni, who backed me 100 percent, even though Lowery had approached me with a tremendous offer to take over Lake Merced Motors.

I then went to Lowery himself. This conversation, I knew, would be a lot more complicated. If I were to turn pro, Lowery would lose a valuable salesman and an asset for the dealership's image.

"I got to show these guys I can play," I told him. "I can't let them think that I'm a choker for the rest of my life."

Lowery wasn't going to give up that easily.

"It's too tough out there," he said. "You're not going to make it."

"I am going to make it!" I responded defiantly. Nothing motivated me more than someone telling me I couldn't do something.

A smile came across Lowery's face. I realized later that he had been testing me and that I had passed.

"I know you're going to make it, Ken," he said. "But if you don't, you will always have a job here."

People assumed that Lowery became my sponsor. I would like to clear up that misconception right now, especially given his problems with the IRS and his involvement in the controversy that resulted in Ward being banned for a year. Lowery gave me a lot of advice, but he never gave me a cent when I began playing professionally. The only thing he had ever paid for was my plane fare to Augusta in 1954. Joe Dey, the executive director of the United States Golf Association (USGA), who would later become the tour commissioner, told me that if I hadn't turned pro, they would've nailed me, just like they nailed Ward. I might have been suspended, and who knows? I might never have been the same player again.

Before I could make it official, however, there was one final tournament to enter, the California Amateur Championship, which I had won once before, over Bud Taylor in 1951. I loved this event, both for its venue, Pebble Beach, and for its caliber of competition.

This time, unlike the U.S. Amateur, there would be no letdown. I moved steadily through the early rounds to secure a berth in the final. My opponent would be Taylor again, which was no surprise. After losing to me and then to Gene Littler in 1953, Taylor, a dentist by trade, had come back to win the event the following two years. About thirty-five hundred people showed up on a damp day to see our highly anticipated, 36-hole duel. The turnout reminded me of the battle between Ward and me for the City Championship.

Taylor started strong, assuming a 1-up advantage after the morning round. He stretched it to 2 with a birdie at the 22nd and was poised to make it 3 on the next hole, the uphill par-3 fifth, when I sailed my tee shot into the bunker. I mishit my bunker shot and found myself with a 22-foot putt for par. A three-hole deficit to Bud Taylor would be almost impossible to make up. But I made the putt and proceeded to birdie three of the next four holes, taking a lead over Taylor that I would not relinquish. I won, 2 and 1, the perfect way to cap my amateur career.

Two months later, on November 28, during a press conference in Lowery's office, I made my announcement.

"I'll never know if I can be a success in golf unless I go on the tour," I said. "I've been in the auto business for a year . . . and in that year, I've tried to tell myself that I should throw aside any thought of turning pro. I know it's a tough way to make a living. I know I face the possibility of bitter disappointment. But every time I tried to convince myself I shouldn't think of turning pro, I found my thoughts reverting again to the job I think I do best—playing golf. It was a nagging feeling."

I felt a tremendous sense of relief, but there was one problem. In the fifties a player was required to wait six months before accepting any official prize money. Today, a hot college player turns pro, hires an agent, and has a lucrative equipment deal before he's even collected his diploma—if he even bothers to collect his diploma. For me it meant selling more cars. Money had to come in from somewhere.

I arrived at another important conclusion: this would be my one and only shot. I took $5,000 out of our savings account, leaving only $5.95. If I were to run through the whole $5,000, I would come home and go back to selling cars, content with the knowledge that I had given professional golf my best shot. No way was I going to be bailed out by a sponsor. I didn't want to owe anybody anything.

Fortunately I didn't have to wait the entire six months to make some money in professional golf. In January, using Byron Nelson clubs and Ben Hogan golf balls—why not associate with the best?— I signed up for two unofficial events, the Crosby at Pebble Beach and the Thunderbird Invitational in Palm Springs. Bing Crosby was very gracious to offer me an invitation, although a few of the other pros grumbled that I was receiving preferential treatment.

I thought of ignoring them but decided I needed to prove myself just like everyone else.

"I'm just starting out on tour and don't want any favors," I told Bing.

"It's my tournament, and I'm inviting you," he said.

"I got to live with these guys out here," I added. "If I can't qualify at Pebble Beach, I don't deserve to be in the tournament."

I qualified, all right, shooting a 69, the lowest score of the day, and tied for fifth in the tournament. The gallery was wonderful, filled with many friends and family members. I'll never forget what the feeling was like, for the first time, to play for money against the top players in the world. I loved it. I followed up two weeks later with a second-place finish in Palm Springs. Altogether, I pocketed over $1,200. Me, a choker? I don't think so.

As a professional I was more serious than ever. I was meticulous about everything. I made sure not to overeat and got at least eight hours of sleep per night. I might have a glass of wine on Sunday night and a Bloody Mary at lunch on Monday. But during tournament week, from Tuesday through Sunday, I wouldn't have a drink.

Before I warmed up, my whole personality began to change. I took my white linen cap, the same kind Hogan wore, off the shelf. The game was on. Was I nervous? You bet I was. I was terrified. Before I teed off, I often went behind a tree and threw up. After the first hole, I was usually fine, playing my normal fast game. I didn't think much of slow players, since I believe that you should start plotting your strategy *before* you arrive at the ball. Hogan gave me a wonderful tip once on how to stay calm under pressure. Grip the club, he said, so that the little finger of your left hand is barely on the club. That took away all the tension.

In April, after my final months with Lowery, I returned to Augusta. I was both excited and apprehensive. Excited because it was The Masters and Augusta National was a course I knew I could handle. Apprehensive because the controversy from 1956 was sure to be brought up again. Still, this was something that I was sure I could handle. Little did I know how tough it was going to be.

"On the tee, Ken Venturi," came the usual introduction, followed by an unusual response: a few people were booing. I was very hurt. "Got any more complaints, crybaby?" was a typical heckle. I tried as much as possible to tune it out, but I wasn't very successful. Any athlete who ever claims he or she doesn't hear the boos is a liar. I managed to maintain enough focus to finish in a tie for 13th, 12 shots behind winner Doug Ford. But I seriously wondered whether I would ever return to The Masters again.

In early May, I teed it up at the Colonial National Invitational, the tournament that Ben Hogan would win a record five times. I wanted to play well for myself, obviously, but also to honor Hogan, who was nearing the twilight of his remarkable career. I didn't play as well as I hoped, shooting four rounds in the 70s, but it was still good enough for 14th place and $531. In June, in the U.S. Open at Inverness in Toledo, Ohio, I finished in the top 10 for the second year in a row, tying for sixth with rounds of 69, 71, 75, and 71.

A week later, I played in the Carling Open Invitational in Flint, Michigan. My six months of waiting were over. Finally, I could earn prize money in official tour events. I was a full-fledged professional golfer. I tied for fourth, picking up my biggest check yet, $1,425.

For a rookie, I was pretty sure of myself. At the 15th hole, in the third round, I holed my approach for an eagle 2. After another good drive at 16, I was probably about 80 yards from the green. Some wise guy in the gallery yelled: "That was a pretty lucky shot you hit there at 15." I looked back at him. "Watch this one," I said. And what do you know? I holed out again. The amazing thing is that I wasn't surprised.

I continued to play well through July and August but wasn't able to string together four good rounds in a row, which is what you need to do to win a tournament on the tour. Finally, at the St. Paul Open Invitational, I shot in the 60s every day, securing my first tour victory and an even bigger check: $2,800. I was focused that week. So focused, in fact, that when Conni congratulated me as I walked up the 72nd fairway, all I could say was "Thanks, lady." I didn't know it was her. I was just as intense with my playing partners. If you asked me after a round what we talked about, I wouldn't be able to remember a thing. My head was completely in the game.

With the triumph in St. Paul, my confidence reached an all-time high. The following week, with 16 of the top 18 money winners in the field at the Miller High Life Open in Milwaukee,

I fired three straight rounds in the 60s to seize a five-stroke advantage. Two wins in a row seemed like a sure bet.

But first, I would have to get past Sam Snead. There was little doubt that Snead, in a group with me and Canada's Al Balding, would attempt to pull every trick he could to thwart me. He enjoyed a well-deserved reputation for turning gamesmanship into an art form. Snead tried first with his clubs, going 2 under par over the first eight holes, while I could do no better than one under par. My lead was dwindling. Snead followed up with Plan B.

As we walked side by side to the ninth tee, he turned to me, lowering his voice.

"Hey, boy, you ain't chokin' again, are you?" he asked, an obvious reference to the final round of the 1956 Masters.

I felt the need to immediately respond. I was a pro now, and knew that the needles came with the territory.

"I'll show you chokin'," I told him.

For the rest of the afternoon I didn't miss a shot. By the time we arrived at the 18th green, I was in full control. All Snead could do was fight with Balding for second place.

Balding went first, from about 35 feet, 2-putting for his par. I was next, 15 feet away. After I putted to within tap-in range, Snead prepared to take his turn, expecting me to mark my ball. That was the protocol, allowing the anticipated winner to have the stage to himself. Only this time, I decided not to follow the protocol. Instead, I crossed my foot over Snead's line and raked the ball back into the hole. This was my message to Snead, who didn't take it very well.

"What the hell were you doin'?" he said, confronting me by the scoring tent.

"Just finishing up," I told him.

"You could have cost me a tie for second place in the tournament. I want to tell you something, boy," he continued, as condescending as ever. "You didn't do the right thing. You should have marked the ball. What do you got to say about that?"

I had plenty to say about that. I got right in his face.

"Sam, let me tell you something," I said. "Remember when we were going to the ninth tee, you said, 'Hey, boy, you chokin' again?' "

"Yeah," he said.

"Well, I want to tell you something," I said. "Don't ever screw with me like that again."

"You got it," Snead replied.

After Milwaukee, Snead never did screw with me again. He would even pass on the lesson he learned to other players. "Don't get Venturi mad," he told them. "Just let him be." Eight months later, at The Masters, I was hanging around with Hogan, Souchak, Burke, Mangrum, and a few others for lunch at the long table upstairs. We were about to play practice rounds when Snead walked in.

"Hey, Ben, how are you?" he said. "You got a game?" I was taken aback. I couldn't remember ever seeing the two of them play a practice round together. I wondered what he had in mind.

"No," Hogan said.

"Would you like a game?" Snead asked.

"Yeah," Hogan replied.

"Well, who you got?" Snead said.

"I'll take Venturi," Hogan said, "and you can take anybody you want." I couldn't look up. To be paid a compliment like that from Ben Hogan, when some of my more accomplished peers were in the same room, was overwhelming.

"I can find an easier game than that," said Snead.

In retrospect, I concede it might have been a mistake to pick Snead as my partner for that fateful, final round of The Masters. There were other players, like Mike Souchak, Gene Littler, or Bob Rosburg, who would have been much better choices. They might have taken the initiative to calm me down when I started to lose control. Who knows? With a more suitable pairing, I might have won. But the loss was no fault of Snead's. Years later, during an awards ceremony at the Waldorf Astoria in New York, I told him so. "Sam, you've taken a lot of heat over the years for what happened at The Masters," I said. "I'd like to tell all of you right now that he was the perfect gentleman."

The victory in Milwaukee was worth $6,000, which again became, by far, the most I ever earned playing golf. I felt on top of the world. Once I made it to the open highway, I rolled down my windows and started to sing as loud as I could. The 80 in Augusta was a distant memory. Thank goodness, I thought. I certainly wouldn't be this happy selling cars. Looking back, I should have driven on to Hartford, the next tour stop. But, instead, I went back to San Francisco. That was a mistake. I was hot. I could have made it three in a row.

There was a lot of money to be made on the course *before* a tournament started. Bo Wininger and I fared particularly well in this department, beating Arnold Palmer and Dow Finsterwald almost every time during practice rounds. We usually played $10 or $20 Nassaus, plus the other types of bets. Wininger had this unbelievable knack for making a crucial putt on the 9th or 18th hole. Too bad we never played together in a Ryder Cup. We would have rolled. Another way to pick up extra dough during the fifties was in the occasional Calcutta. For the best example, fast-forward a year to Palm Springs, when I played in the Thunderbird Invitational.

Early in the week, Chauncey Needham, a well-to-do business-man, told me he had purchased me in the Calcutta and that I would receive a piece of the action. (A Calcutta is when people bid for players, like in an auction. So, let's say a person bids $200 and gets Gene Littler, and Littler then wins the tournament. That person would receive a certain percentage of the Calcutta pot. Those who picked the second- or third-place finishers would usually get something, too. Players did not take part, but the amateur might come to them and give them a share, or let them know ahead of time). I knew from the start I was playing for a lot more than the $1,500 first prize. No worries. I had grown up quite a bit in the eight years since I played Martin Stanovich in the City Championship. I was now equipped to deal with the pressure of knowing that someone else's money was on the line. As proof, I went out and won the tournament. After I accepted the $1,500 and a new, powder blue, four-seat Ford Thunderbird, worth $4,500, Needham handed me an envelope. "Here's your part of the Calcutta," he said. I put it in my pocket. When I opened it in the locker room alone, inside were 10 $1,000 bills. I had never seen that kind of cash before.

Not every Calcutta story came with a happy ending. Fast-forward again, this time to the 1960 Crosby at Pebble Beach. Some guy I had never met before approached me before the tournament started.

"I bought you in the Calcutta," he said. "You win, I'll give you $5,000."

"That's fine," I responded. I was a little ticked off. This guy had the nerve to talk to me when my game face was already on. I always felt the hour or two before any tournament round was *my* time.

Nonetheless, I didn't want to miss out. Five thousand dollars was five thousand dollars.

"Show up at the 18th green come Sunday," I told him.

Come Sunday, when I did win the Crosby, there were tons of people at the 18th green to congratulate me. This guy, of course, was not one of them. I never saw him again.

Win or lose, the tour was a wonderful place to be. We were like a gang of gypsies, traveling in a caravan across America, staying at the same motels and dining at the same restaurants. We didn't go from the range to dinner with our agent or to the gym with our trainer. We instead shared with each other the highs—and, too often, the lows—of a game that we loved. We were in this together. Did we want to win as much money as possible? Absolutely. Was it *all* about money, like it seems to be for so many of today's players? Absolutely not.

In 1957, there wasn't much more I could have accomplished. In 16 tournaments, I finished with two victories and recorded 10 top 10s. My poorest performance was a tie for 29th in the World Championship of Golf. Voted *Golf Digest's* Rookie of the Year, I was the tour's 10th-leading money winner with $18,762 in official earnings. The 10th-leading money winner today earns over $3 million.

I was only getting started.

Chapter Eight

MORE AGONY AT AUGUSTA

In the winter of 1957, I knew I couldn't afford to be complacent. Nothing is guaranteed in this unpredictable game. All one has to do is look at the terrific players who suddenly and mysteriously lose their skills, never returning to their prior form. The only guarantee was that I would keep working hard. If I ever needed inspiration, I opened my wallet and read the two Ben Hogan sayings I carried with me:

> *Every day you miss practicing will take you one day longer to be good.*
> *There isn't enough daylight in any one day to practice all the shots you need to.*

But how often you practice wasn't the only thing that mattered. One needed to practice smart, which is why I kept records of certain shots I hit in tournament competition. Back then, unlike today, there was an off-season. We were done, essentially, by mid-October, giving us almost three full months to tinker with our games away from the tour. To stay sharp, I often worked two or three hours a day on an individual club, hitting shot after shot to maintain the proper rhythm.

Practicing at home with no gallery and no pressure was only a start. I always believed that the best way to test the effectiveness of swing alterations was during tournament competition. My winter's hard work paid off in a hurry. I tied for 10th in Los Angeles, finished 3rd at the Crosby, and then won in Palm Springs. My next stop was Phoenix.

Over the first three rounds at Phoenix Country Club, I kept up my excellent play, shooting rounds of 70, 68, and 66. On the 17th tee during the final round, I showed once again how much I believed in myself. Asking for a towel from my caddie, I started to clean my shoes. A writer from the wire services was following our group.

"What are you doing?" he asked.

"My shoes are dirty," I said. "I need to get them ready for the presentation."

"The presentation? What are you talking about? You still have to birdie the last two holes to win," the writer continued.

"So?"

On 17, I hit my approach to about one foot from the hole. On 18, a par-5, I got home in two and proceeded to 2-putt for another birdie, winning by a shot over Jay Hebert and Walter Burkemo. My shoes, incidentally, were clean for the presentation.

In Phoenix a number of players complained about the course, and they had a point. The greens were burned out due to a chemical reaction, and the tees were almost without any grass. When the press asked me for my feelings, I did not complain.

Everyone, after all, has to play the same course. Come Sunday night, someone had to win the tournament, and it might as well be me.

I've always contended that the ones who complained the most were players who had psyched themselves out of winning the tournament.

Two more solid performances followed—a tie for 4th in Tucson and a 10th-place finish in Houston—giving me six top 10s in six starts.

I made it seven for seven in Baton Rouge, winning by four strokes. What I recall most about that triumph was that I put together four straight 69s. I played very well on a narrow, demanding course. I felt like I was in a position to do anything I wanted.

I almost won a week later in New Orleans, shooting a 66 on the last day, but Billy Casper, a superb putter, tied me with a 20-footer for birdie on the 72nd hole. Casper holed another long one for par on the first playoff hole and sank a 30-footer for an eagle 3 to beat me on the second playoff hole, a par-5.

I had been sitting pretty, on the green in three, about a foot and a half away. But nobody ever laid down for me. Someone always seemed to pull off a miraculous shot to deprive me of apparent victory.

A week later, in Pensacola, Doug Ford made a 53-foot putt on 18 to win by two shots. I think Greg Norman and I have a lot in common.

No matter. I was playing the best golf of my life, leading the money list with more than 15 grand, and it couldn't have come at a more appropriate time. Spring arrived, which means only one thing in the world of professional golf: The Masters.

I was going back, of course. Any thought of staying away, due to the negative public reaction in 1957, had been dismissed long ago. I was no choker, and I was no quitter. I was a grown-up who could handle the boos. Besides, in the wake of my wonderful play—I finished first or second in five of the previous seven events—the golf writers had installed me as the favorite to win the green jacket. I was determined to prove them right.

I didn't waste any time, shooting an opening 68 to assume a one-stroke lead over a quartet of players that included Jimmy Demaret. Arnold Palmer and Cary Middlecoff were two back, while Fred Hawkins, Art Wall Jr., Claude Harmon, Byron Nelson, and Billy Maxwell were in a group three behind. I still detected a scattering of boos, but, for the most part, the gallery seemed more than willing to afford me a second chance. With warm temperatures and almost no wind the course was playing much easier than usual. In all, 17 players broke par. I knew I had better take advantage. I was especially effective on the greens, requiring only 28 putts.

Friday was another day entirely. The course took advantage of me. I went out with a 4-over-par 40, which included a very untimely double bogey at the par-5 8th. My fourth shot looked perfect but hit the flagstick and, unluckily, caromed back about 40 feet. I 3-putted. I was discouraged enough to be playing that poorly, but what disturbed me even more were some harsh words from a few of the "patrons." I had allowed myself to believe that the worst was over.

"I'm glad you shot 40," someone remarked at the turn. "I hope you shoot another 40. You chokin' again?"

I was reminded of what Snead said to me in Milwaukee. I vowed to respond the same way, with my clubs.

I rallied with a 32 on the back nine. At 18, I lined up a 20-foot birdie putt that broke from right to left. Even before the putt dropped, I threw my hat to the ground.

"You son of a bitch," I said under my breath. "Take that, you crummy bums. I'll show you chokin'."

Despite the up-and-down even-par 72, I was still on top at the halfway mark, by one stroke over Maxwell and Billy Joe Patton, and by two strokes over Bo Wininger and Stan Leonard. Palmer, Wall, Middlecoff, and Snead were among those who trailed by three.

I didn't fare nearly as well on Saturday, firing a pair of 37s to fall three behind Palmer, who rallied with a 68. Tied with Palmer was the incredible, 45-year-old Snead. Sunday promised to be an important day for Palmer, yet to win a major himself—yet to become, well, Arnold Palmer. I believed that it could be an important day for me, as well. I would be paired with Palmer, which gave me plenty of confidence. After all the matches with Wininger and myself against him and Finsterwald, I felt like I could handle the case.

During the night, there was a heavy downpour. No big deal, I thought. After all, everybody would be dealing with the same soggy conditions. It would, however, turn out to be a very big deal. Early on, Palmer and I were notified that Snead double-bogeyed the first hole. He would not be a factor. The tournament, it became increasingly clear to us, would come down to Palmer against me. Which was exactly what I wanted.

On the front nine, I shot a 35, Palmer a 36. The lead was down to two. On the difficult par-4 10th, Palmer finished with a bogey. Now the margin was only one. The momentum was all mine.

After we each parred the 11th, I hit first on the always treacherous par-3 12th, sending the ball to the back edge of the green, about 20 feet from the cup. That was the smart play, especially with the traditional Sunday pin placement far right, and only a few yards behind the water. You don't ever want to mess with the 12th pin in the final round.

Palmer followed by sailing his approach over the green, about a foot and a half from the bunker. Though his ball was embedded in the bank, it seemed he would, under the rules, be entitled to a free drop.

But Arthur Lacey, the rules official, saw the situation differently. "It's not embedded," he told Palmer. "It's only half embedded."

"Half embedded?" I said. "That's like being half pregnant. You're either pregnant or you're not."

Palmer and Lacey continued to argue. Concerned that I would lose my concentration, I told them I would putt out. After barely missing my birdie attempt, I rejoined Palmer and Lacey to catch the rest of their discussion. Nothing was resolved. I sat on my bag with Mutt, my caddie. This matter was obviously going to take longer than I thought. While I sided with Palmer's interpretation, I realized I might capitalize from his misfortune.

Finally, an angry Palmer played the shot. Not surprisingly, he flubbed the chip and the ball did not even reach the putting surface. He hit the next one five feet past the hole but then missed the putt, making a five. The two-shot swing put me in the lead for the first time since early in the third round. Two years after my memorable collapse, I was on my way toward a memorable comeback.

Only Palmer wasn't ready to give up on the 12th hole just yet.

"I didn't like your ruling," he said, glaring at Lacey. "I'm going to play a provisional ball." (He was really playing what is called a "second ball.") "You can't do that," I told him. "You have to declare a second *before* you hit your first one. Suppose you had chipped in with the other ball? Would you still be playing a second?"

But Palmer had his mind made up. I turned to Mutt.

"Mutt, we got 'em now," I said, knowing Palmer was in violation of the rules. "It doesn't make any difference what he does with this ball."

Palmer didn't say another word. He took the drop. The ball rolled toward the hole two times in a row, allowing him to place it. This time, with a better sense of the speed of the green, he almost chipped it in, tapping in for par.

We proceeded to the 13th tee. By the time we arrived, I was no longer angry. If anything, I was amused. I was certain the officials, once they checked the rule book, wouldn't give Palmer the second ball. The five, not three, would stand, and so, too, would my one-stroke advantage.

At 13, Palmer outdrove me by a yard or two. Hitting first, I made the smart play again, laying up with a 4 iron. With the lead, I wasn't going to do anything stupid . . . or so I thought. But then I committed a big mental blunder, and I didn't even have a club in my hands. Even now, the mere memory makes me ill.

Palmer, preparing to hit an iron to lay up, had stopped and turned to me.

"You know, they're going to give me a five back there at 12, aren't they?" he asked.

"You bet your ass they're going to give you a five," I responded.

That was the worst possible thing I could have said. There were so many better answers, such as: "I don't know, Arnold, we'll have to see when we get in," or "You never really know with rules officials," or "Oh, I'm sure they'll give you a three." At the very least, I should have said nothing. For many years, because of my stammering, I was the man to give short answers. I could have really used one in this situation.

Why was my response so stupid? Because, by telling him that he was sure to get a double bogey at 12, I believe I helped convince him to put the iron back in his bag and go for the green in two. He might have played it more conservatively if he thought he was still in the lead. In any case, I know I shouldn't have tortured myself for all these years. Knowing the aggressive way Palmer played the game, he probably would have gone for it anyway.

Lo and behold, the gamble paid off. His approach bounced on the small neck in front of the green just over the water. A few yards to the left or a few yards to the right and his ball would have gone in the creek. Instead, it came to a rest about 20 feet from the cup. Palmer, of course, would make the putt for an eagle. After a wonderful wedge, I tapped in for a birdie, convinced I was still tied for the lead. I was still pretty confident I could win.

But, walking up the fairway at 14, I saw Bill Kerr, a member of Augusta National and one of Cliff Roberts' assistants. Kerr, wearing his green coat, was running down the middle of the fairway. I soon found out the cause of his exuberance.

"They gave Arnold a 3 at 12," Kerr shouted. "They gave Arnold a 3 at 12."

The gallery went crazy. So did I, for a different reason. This simply was not happening, I kept reassuring myself. Kerr must have received the wrong information.

"Get the hell off the fairway," I told him. "You don't belong in the fairway."

Palmer turned to me, asking, "What do you think?" I didn't answer. Not this time.

I tried not to worry about it, figuring I would deal with the situation when we finished the round. But it was no use. My concentration was shattered for good.

I proceeded to 3-putt 14, 3-putt the par-5 15th after getting on the green in two, and 3-putt 16. Palmer hung on to win by one stroke over Doug Ford and Fred Hawkins. I tied for fourth, two shots back.

In the scoring tent, I gave Palmer another chance.

"You're signing an incorrect card," I told him.

"No, I'm not," he said. "The ruling was made."

Nonetheless, the way I figured it, the matter was still far from over. After signing my scorecard, I went to see Mr. Roberts. All I was trying to do at this point was protect the field. I no longer had a chance to win, but I strongly believed that Ford and Hawkins should, at the very least, be given an opportunity to fight it out between themselves.

I started to lay out the whole sequence of events for Mr. Roberts, that Palmer, under the rules, was required to declare that he was going to play a second ball before hitting the first one.

I was wasting my breath. Mr. Roberts wasn't interested in fact. In his mind, he already knew the facts.

Becoming more frustrated by the second, I asked that Mr. Roberts bring in Arthur Lacey. Lacey would make things right.

Only one problem: Lacey, I was told, had already left the golf course, and there was no way to track him down. There were no cell phones in 1958. A pretty quick exit from the premises, don't you think? I certainly don't have any evidence that Mr. Roberts, anxious to avoid controversy, made sure Lacey got off the grounds in a hurry, but it sure looked fishy. The one person who could clear up the whole mess was nowhere to be found. (I wrote a letter to Lacey, saying, "I'm sorry we didn't get together before the tournament was over, and I'm sure you'll agree that it was not the right ruling, and hopefully we'll see each other some time." I did not receive a response.)

Then I said, to Mr. Roberts: "Bring in Arnold. Rules are rules."

By now, Roberts had listened long enough. He wasn't going to bring in anyone.

"I don't need to know the rules," he said. "I make the rules." There was no doubt. Even the great Bobby Jones, on matters pertaining to the actual running of the golf tournament, deferred to Cliff Roberts.

"I told Cliff the ruling was wrong," Jones told me a few years later. "But I was overruled. I always believed you were right. I'm so sorry."

I thought, briefly, about finding the press to make my case, but I quickly reasoned that such a plea would also get nowhere. If anything, going public would damage my fragile image even further. "Look at that Venturi," they would write. "He's always complaining about something."

What took place at the 12th hole, to be sure, would never happen on today's PGA Tour. There are too many observers—writers, announcers, spotters, rules officials, and cameras—at every tournament to let any infraction go unnoticed. And in the rare case in which they were to miss a violation, believe me, a viewer lounging on his couch in Flint, Michigan, would call the networks in no time to make sure the error was rectified.

The viewer in Flint didn't see Palmer and me play the 12th hole in the 1958 Masters. Television coverage in those days wasn't comprehensive like it is today. Too bad for Doug Ford (the 1957 Masters winner) and for Fred Hawkins, who would never win a major. They were robbed.

As the years went on, even some prominent experts in the game got it wrong, such as former commissioner Joe Dey. Dey wrote an article about the matter for *Golf Digest* magazine in 1983, not knowing the exact chronology of events. When I provided him with the whole explanation, he felt horrible and apologized profusely. Other publications have indicated that Palmer acted properly, citing the rule that allowed a free lift from an embedded ball. I don't disagree. All I'm saying is that Palmer made improper use of the second ball.

I've never gotten over what happened at the 12th hole. Why didn't I come forward sooner? I couldn't, not with my responsibilities and loyalties to CBS. The network needed to maintain a good relationship with Augusta National. If I had spoken out, that relationship might have been irrevocably harmed, and CBS might have lost coverage of The Masters. I couldn't take that risk. But I've retired now from CBS.

I'll start with Palmer. First, like so many others, I am extremely grateful for the contribution he's made to the game. I can't imagine where golf would be without him. Also, regardless of what I believe took place at the 12th hole at Augusta National 46 long years ago, it should not take anything away from that contribution. The game has never known a more deserving ambassador.

At the same time, nobody, not even Palmer, is bigger than the game. I firmly believe that he did wrong, and that he knows that I know he did wrong. That is why, to this day, it has left me with an uncomfortable feeling.

Arnold has never brought up 1958, and neither have I. I understand. The past is the past. What I don't understand is his still believing that he was right, as he said in his 2002 book, *Playing by the Rules*.

If people don't know which interpretation to accept, his or mine, all I ask is that they look up the rule about hitting a second ball and decide for themselves. I have nothing against him personally. But we all know the rules.

My feelings about this matter, at least among close friends, have been no secret. Which is why, in the 2002 Masters, CBS producer Lance Barrow was worried what I might say when Palmer made what was billed then as his farewell appearance (though he came back a year later). Barrow had nothing to worry about. I was as professional as ever, praising Palmer for what he's meant to the game. "How about that applause?" Jim Nantz said, as Palmer approached the 18th green. "They are honoring a man," I said, "who has won four green jackets."

Only once did I let Palmer know exactly how I felt. The scene was the post-tournament ceremony at the 1960 Masters. Palmer birdied the final two holes to beat me by a shot. He leaned over to me, saying softly: "I wish it could have been you. I wish you had won."

"It's two years too late," I said.

In the spring of 1977, I was playing Augusta National's par-3 course a week after the tournament when I ran into Cliff Roberts. Jack Rodgers, who was my best friend, was with me. Beau was in the hospital for a cancer checkup.

Roberts was going for a walk on the old 9th hole of the par-3 course with Jerry Franklin, an Augusta National member.

"Is that you, Ken?" Roberts said.

"Yes, Cliff," I responded. I always called him Cliff because, after the 1958 ruling, I had lost some respect for the man. I stopped calling him Mr. Roberts.

"Can I see you?" he said, telling Franklin he needed some privacy.

Sure, I told him, asking Jack Rodgers to give me a few minutes.

"Ken," he said, after inquiring into Beau's health, "I want to congratulate you for the way you've handled yourself, the respect you have for this golf course and for this tournament. You are a credit to the game. You never said a single word about the episode at 12."

"Thank you," I said.

He then got to the real point he wanted to make.

"I want to ask for your forgiveness," he continued. "When I made the ruling in 1958, it was wrong. I'm ashamed of myself. I made the ruling because of what you said in 1956. I know now that wasn't Ken Venturi, not the Ken Venturi we all know and love. If you can somehow find it in your heart to forgive me, I would certainly appreciate it. I now wish you could have been a Masters champion."

"Mr. Roberts," I said, now willing to afford him the proper respect, "you've soothed a lot of wounds. I'm glad you know the real story, because I never said those things in 1956."

We said our good-byes. I never saw Cliff Roberts again. About six months later, near the lake on the club's par-3 course, he committed suicide. I felt sad. I truly believe he was very sorry about what transpired in 1958.

In the early eighties, there was one more apology, and from a most surprising source. Again, ironically enough, I was with Jack

Rodgers at Augusta, this time walking down the 11th fairway late in the afternoon on the Sunday before The Masters. I was able to play on the weekends before the galleries were allowed in on Monday. Suddenly, it occurred to me that I had seen this caddie before, but I couldn't quite place him.

"Where do I know you from?" I finally asked him.

"Mr. Ken, I'm Ironman," the caddie said.

Why, of course, *Ironman*, Palmer's caddie for years at Augusta. Instantly a flood of memories came back, some good, some not good. We exchanged small talk for a few minutes, but as we approached the 12th green, I could no longer avoid the obvious reference.

"Ironman," I said, "will you ever forget this hole?"

It was a light, friendly remark, or so I thought. Within seconds, I realized that I had touched a painful part of his past.

"No, Mr. Ken, I will never forget this hole," he said. "I felt so bad. I told Mr. Palmer, 'You're doing the wrong thing. You can't do that. It's illegal. You got a five there.' He said, 'I'll get the ruling myself.' I hope you do forgive me, Mr. Ken."

He then provided a piece of the story that had been missing.

"I tried to tell them what happened when I got inside the clubhouse, that I thought what Mr. Palmer did was wrong," Ironman said, adding that he was scared that he would never be able to work again if he discussed the matter further.

I could not believe my ears. Ironman started to cry.

"Please forgive me, Mr. Ken," he said.

We hardly spoke the rest of the round. What else was there to say? But when we finished I told him how I felt. I was very glad that Jack Rodgers, who died a few years later, was there to be my witness. He had always believed me, but having him hear the truth firsthand made a big difference. I didn't care who else knew, as long as my best friend knew.

"Ironman, I am so proud of you," I said. "You did the right thing. You should have no regrets. Your family and you are the most important thing. What counts more to me is that I have you as a friend."

I gave him $100. Ironman walked away, still in tears.

I never saw him again.

Chapter Nine

THIRD TIME IS NO CHARM

The loss at Augusta in 1958 hurt just as much as the loss in 1956. I was in great position on the back nine again and lost again.

Not until a month later, at the Colonial tournament in Fort Worth, was I able to regroup. I played a wonderful tournament, though Tommy Bolt edged me by a shot. At 13 Bolt made a key 30-foot putt. He played very solidly the rest of the way. Nobody, I repeat, ever laid down for me.

Bolt was truly an amazing character. I was paired with him once when he 3-putted the 11th hole. He walked from the green right into the clubhouse. I swear this is a completely true story. I'll say one thing for the guy: there are very few players in my era, or in today's era, whom I would go out of my way to follow on the course. Tommy Bolt was one of them. He possessed such a beautiful swing.

Finally, in August at Gleneagles, just outside Chicago, I won again. Despite my disappointment at Augusta, 1958 was a very successful season—four victories and $36,268 in official earnings, third on the money list. An argument could be made that I was the best player in the game. I was also making some money away from the course. I signed an endorsement deal with U.S. Royal, one of the most prominent ball companies at the time. In the process, I earned the permanent respect of Ben Hogan.

Hogan was hoping I would sign a contract with his company, or at least listen to his offer.

"Please call me first," he said.

"Ben, I promise I will not sign anything until I call you first," I told him.

Some time later, in Eddie Lowery's office in San Francisco, I entered into negotiations with John Sproul, head of U.S. Royal. He was offering me $25,000 plus bonuses, a tremendous proposal. I was ready to sign on the dotted line, but I told Sproul that I had to talk to Hogan first. Trouble was, I couldn't track him down right away.

Sproul left for lunch. When he returned, I still hadn't reached Hogan. Sproul was becoming a little antsy.

"Just sign this now because I have to go," he said. "Tell Hogan what you did when he calls."

I would not do that. I gave Hogan my word, and to me, my word meant a lot more than $25,000.

We finally reached Hogan the next morning. Sproul got on the line. "I told him he could lose the contract," Sproul said to Hogan, "and he said, 'If that's the case, that's the way it is.' This guy told me that he had given you his word that he wouldn't sign anything until he spoke with you first."

He handed the phone back to me. "Hogan wants to speak to you," Sproul said.

"I can't offer you as much money as U.S. Royal," said Hogan, whose proposal was $5,000 with no bonuses. "But Ken, I want you to remember one thing. If there is anything that you ever need, you call me. You will always play with me."

Hogan kept his word, as well. I would always play with him.

Over the winter, I went through my standard postmortem, tracking what part of my game worked and what part of my game didn't work. I was far from satisfied. On my resume, there was still no major championship, the true distinction that separates the good from the great players in the game. I expected better things in 1959.

The season started, as usual, at Rancho Park in Los Angeles. I didn't fare too well the first three days, shooting rounds of 72, 71, and 72, falling eight shots behind the leader, Art Wall Jr. Frustrated with my performance, I went to the range after my round, but I was still unable to identify the problem in my swing. The answers, if there were any, would have to come another day.

Or maybe not. Back in my hotel room, I took a few practice swings. Suddenly I felt like I was on to something. Taking a bunch of balls out of my bag, I opened the sliding door and started to hit iron shots off the rug, over the balcony, over the cars, and onto an adjacent empty lot. All it took was about a dozen swings to figure out what was wrong with my mechanics. I closed the door, finally content, and went to sleep.

The next day I went out and shot 63 to win the golf tournament. The weather was cold, windy, and rainy—my kind of weather, San Francisco weather. I shot a 30 on the front nine, which included back-to-back eagles at 8 and 9, before Wall had even teed off, and closed with five straight 3s to win by two. The next lowest score that day was 69.

Winning another tournament wasn't that noteworthy. I had won six times before. What was noteworthy was the way I won it, showing courage, determination, and the ability to fight back from a huge deficit. I sure had come a long way since the 80 in Augusta. Of course, in the minds of some writers, I hadn't come far enough. They were never going to let me forget Augusta and what they assumed I said that day at the airport in San Francisco.

The victory in Los Angeles put me in line for more lucrative endorsements, but I was never the type to jump at any offer, no matter how much money was put on the table. A tobacco company, for example, came to me the morning after my victory to see if I would smoke a cigarette for one of their advertisements. I told them I didn't smoke. No problem, they said. All I had to do was hold a cigarette in my hand and say: "It couldn't be done," an obvious reference to my 63. No thanks, I told them. Believe me, it was not easy turning down the money, especially when they upped the offer from $7,500 to $15,000 to $20,000, but my image was more important than my bank account. I didn't want the kids of America thinking that, to play golf, you needed to smoke. Byron Nelson told me the one decision in his entire career that he regretted was doing an ad for a cigarette company. I know I would have felt the same way.

I thought the win in L.A. would be the start of a banner year for me. It wasn't. Between January and April, in eight starts, I was able to record only two top 10s—a second at the Thunderbird and a fifth in Pensacola. Maybe I needed to hit more balls off my hotel balcony. I wasn't too discouraged. The Masters was coming up, an opportunity to turn my year around in a hurry and make amends for the tough setbacks in 1956 and 1958. But this time there would be no collapse on the weekend. There would be no weekend, period. I shot rounds of 75 and 76, missing the cut. Wall prevailed by a shot over Middlecoff.

The rest of the year was fairly uneventful, except for my second straight triumph at Gleneagles in Chicago, by a stroke over Johnny Pott. I played one of my all-time great shots that week, taking a gamble with my wedge by aiming over a bunker with very little green to work with. The gamble paid off. Afterward, I was so excited I approached Wininger.

"Bo, I've never done much celebrating," I said. "Will you show me how to celebrate?"

Sure, he said. I then went to Johnny Pott and his wife, Mary Rose, to see if they would join us at the Pump Room in downtown Chicago for dinner. "We would love to," they said. We ran up a pretty expensive bill, especially for the late fifties, but I didn't care. We were having a wonderful time.

The biggest news in 1959 took place at home in August, with the birth of our second son, Timothy Frederick. I can't say that Conni and I had suddenly fallen in love. Like many modern couples, I suppose we had settled into a stable routine that worked for both of us. Home was a place for me to unwind after weeks on the road, and Conni was able to buy all the things that she wanted. We did well enough to move from Westlake to Hillsborough, one of San Francisco's most exclusive suburbs.

I did not play my best for the remainder of the 1959 season, tying for fifth at the PGA Championship in Minneapolis but picking up only two other top 10s.

Even so, for the year, I pocketed $25,887, finishing 10th on the money list. If this was going to go down as my "bad" year, I was in store for one heck of a career.

Soon it was a new year, a new decade, and I was back in good form. After a so-so performance in Los Angeles, I prevailed at Pebble Beach, shooting a final-round 77 to defeat Julius Boros and Tommy Jacobs by three shots. The weather was so miserable, even by Pebble standards, that Bing Crosby gave serious thought to canceling the tournament. For example, I hit a full 3 iron on the short, par-3 7th hole, when the right play is usually a wedge or 9 iron. I didn't win again over the next three months but seemed to be in contention every week—fifth in Palm Springs, fifth in Phoenix, fifth in Pensacola, third in St. Petersburg, and ninth in Sarasota. I was getting hot at the perfect time. Augusta was next.

The experts predicted the battle would come down to Arnold Palmer and myself, just as they had predicted Harvie Ward and I would square off for the City Championship four years earlier. The experts were right again.

Palmer was on an even more impressive run, already holding four victories—Palm Springs, San Antonio, Baton Rouge, and Pensacola. Three of them came in a row. He was as motivated as ever, determined to make up for his poor play down the stretch in the 1959 Masters, when he finished third behind Wall and Middlecoff. I was also motivated. What happened to me in 1958, not to mention 1956, was very much on my mind.

I got off to a tremendous start, shooting a 31 on the front, putting myself in position to post an extremely low score. But just as rapidly, I lost it on the back, getting around in 42, the same woeful number I recorded on the back nine in 1956. I double-bogeyed 12, followed with a few more miscues, and then took three shots from near the green to bogey 18. I could almost hear the echoes of Sam Snead: "Boy, are you chokin' again?" Adding to my disappointment was the fact that Palmer was in the lead with a brilliant 67. Spotting him six strokes on the first day was not my plan.

But even Palmer, I figured (or at least hoped), couldn't maintain such a torrid pace, not on Augusta's typically tricky greens. I was right. He bogeyed three of the first eight holes in the second round, finishing with a 1-over 73. Meanwhile, I rebounded with a 69, closing the deficit to only two. I was back in the game. I gained another stroke on him in the third round, setting the stage for Sunday. Would it finally be my moment at Augusta National?

It sure looked that way in the early going. Paired with Dow Finsterwald, I birdied three of the first six holes, while Palmer went in the opposite direction. When he bogeyed the fourth hole, I was on top.

Coming home, I 3-putted 14 again, just as I had in 1956 and 1958. No wonder I didn't like that hole. At 16, I was in danger of dropping another stroke when I sent my approach into the back right bunker. The pin was in the back right, leaving me almost no green to work with. If I were to hit it a hair too hard, I would run it off the green, setting up a good chance to make five and lose the tournament. Byron Nelson, in the 15th tower with Cliff Roberts, told me later that Roberts had said, "Nobody can get this up and down in two." Nelson dared to disagree.

"You're looking at the only man who can do it," he told Roberts. "He's the best bunker player I ever saw."

Thankfully, I made Nelson look good, blasting it out to a few inches short of the hole, dead center. To this day, I cannot believe the ball stopped.

After a safe par on 17, I headed to 18 with more than Palmer to worry about. I was tied with Finsterwald, a wonderful, if underrated, player. After a perfect drive, I hit my approach to within about 15 feet. I wanted to make the birdie, naturally, but, facing a slick downhill putt, I needed to protect against making five. A par would put me in the clubhouse at 5 under. The pressure would be on Finsterwald, who was eight feet away for par, and Palmer, who stood at 4 under through 15.

Mission accomplished: I lagged to within six inches. Finsterwald then missed his putt. He was out of it. Palmer was the only one who could catch me.

He was certainly making it hard on himself. At 16, he faced a 30-foot uphill putt for birdie. At that time, players on the green were allowed to leave the pin in the cup without incurring a penalty. Palmer, as aggressive as ever, killed his first putt. Another bogey would be extremely costly, forcing Palmer to close with two birdies to get a playoff. Lo and behold, his putt hit the flagstick, leaving him with an easy two-footer for par. Billy Casper, his playing partner, later said: "If the ball hadn't hit the pin, it would have gone in the bunker. It was going a mile a minute."

So were my thoughts, as a matter of fact, as I spoke to the media briefly after the round. I then went to Cliff Roberts' cottage to watch Palmer play the last two holes. Byron and Louise Nelson were already there.

By the time I arrived, Palmer was walking toward the 17th green. He lined up a 35-foot birdie attempt. Because of the speed, I figured there was a very realistic possibility that he would 3-putt. The 17th green at Augusta is one of the hardest in the world to figure out. So what did Palmer do? After backing away from it a few times, he made the putt, of course, sparking one of the loudest roars I had ever heard at Augusta National. With his unorthodox, go-for-broke style, he was the people's favorite, on the way to permanent status as a genuine American icon.

I was stunned. Could this actually be happening to me again? Was I destined for yet another heartbreaking defeat?

I remember having a strange thought. I was hoping that Palmer wouldn't birdie or bogey the 18th hole. I felt my victory would be tainted if he were to bogey, and after what took place between us in 1958, I wanted the championship to be decided, once and for all, in an 18-hole playoff, best man wins. I was confident I could be the best man.

Palmer hit an excellent drive at 18 and followed with a superb approach to within about six feet. When I saw where the ball ended up, I walked out of the cottage by myself. I didn't have to watch. The roar, even louder than the last one, told me everything I needed to know.

Suddenly, coming up just short for the third time in five years, all the powerful emotions I had buried for so long came pouring out. I was heartbroken. Why me? Losing in 1960 was even tougher to swallow than the losses in 1956 and 1958. This was supposed to have been my turn. My mom told me never to cry in defeat, but this was the one time I couldn't help myself. Fortunately, Byron and Louise Nelson were able to comfort me. I certainly needed it.

There was no 80 this time around, no incorrect ruling. Yet I did not win The Masters. Little did I know that I would never come close again. I would never become a member of that exclusive club, Masters champions.

After taking a few weeks off, I went back on the road, putting together a series of solid performances, though nothing spectacular.

In the U.S. Open at Cherry Hills Country Club in Denver, I was never a factor and finished well behind Palmer, who captured his second straight major with a remarkable final-round 65, solidifying his standing as the best golfer in the world.

Driving the green on the par-4 first hole was one of the game's signature moments. Palmer was challenged that week by a 20-year-old amateur from Columbus, Ohio. Everyone who was at Cherry Hills knew this amateur would be something special. His name was Jack Nicklaus. The 1960 Open was also the tournament where Ben Hogan backed his third shot into the water at the par-5 17th, squandering his last good chance to win a record fifth Open. The shot, Hogan told me years later in a rare interview at Shady Oaks, would stay with him for a long time.

"I found myself waking up at night," Hogan said. "There isn't a month that goes by that it doesn't cut my guts out."

In late August at the Milwaukee Open I picked up my first victory since the Crosby. Maybe the setback at The Masters took a lot out of me, or maybe I just wasn't getting the breaks. Either way, the year that had started off with so much promise did not produce what I expected.

I earned $41,230 to finish second on the money list, and collected 18 top 10s in 24 starts—the kind of statistics that would have satisfied most players. Yet I had won only two tournaments and, again, no majors.

By my standards, 1960 wasn't good enough.

Chapter Ten

LOSING MY GRIP

As the 1961 season got under way, there was no reason to believe that anything would change, that I wouldn't, once again, be one of the top two or three players in the game. I was, for a few months anyway, still in my twenties. My most productive years were surely in the future. As brilliantly as Palmer had performed in 1960, I was convinced that I could match, if not surpass, him. I started with three straight top 10s, but in the final round at Palm Springs, my fourth appearance, I received the first signal that this was going to be a difficult year.

Going to the 15th hole, I was in contention, but my tee shot went right, perhaps even out of bounds. I put another ball down to hit a provisional, just in case. A split second before impact, a marshal about 10 yards away yelled: "You're in bounds. You're all right." The distraction caused me to hit my second shot even further off line, way left this time and definitely out of bounds. Yet, figuring that my original shot was safe, there was no problem.

Actually, there *was* a problem, a huge problem. The marshal had spoken too soon. An official told me my first tee shot might be out of bounds after all. After I walked all the way to the ball, they used a string to determine that it was out of bounds by an inch, a lousy inch. I was forced to walk all the way back to the tee to hit a third drive. I was beginning to wonder if I would ever finish this hole. That ball found the fairway, but I was lying five and hadn't even reached the green. I finished with an eight, leading to a 76 and ending any chance of winning the tournament. I tied for fifth.

Two months later, after a few more uneven performances, I arrived at Augusta, an opportunity for redemption. Some opportunity. I finished 11th, failing to record a single round in the 60s. If that weren't disappointing enough, the green jacket went to Gary Player when Palmer double-bogeyed the 72nd hole. My first thought, going back to 1960, was: why me? Why couldn't Palmer have doubled 18 *then*?

I recovered quickly. Two weeks later I played my best golf in a long time, shooting rounds of 70, 70, 68, and 68 at the Houston Classic. I was on the verge of certain victory until Jay Hebert, the latest spoiler, birdied three of the last four holes to tie me. We started over in an 18-hole playoff but remained tied again. On to sudden death. I lost, of course, when Hebert birdied the next hole. In my career, I was 0 for 3 in playoffs. I can provide no explanation. Nonetheless, my performance in Houston gave me a reason to be encouraged, to believe that the season could still be salvaged.

Then came San Antonio and the Texas Open Invitational. I was paired with Jimmy Demaret and Tommy Bolt. When we arrived at the 5th hole, I hit my ball into an earth crack, an opening caused by the heat and dryness.

"What do I do?" I asked my playing partners.

"We drop out of that," Demaret assured me. "We've always dropped out of earth cracks."

If Jimmy Demaret, a three-time Masters champion, said I was entitled to a free drop, that was good enough for me. I took the drop, went on to shoot 67, and didn't think about the earth crack again.

Until the final round, that is. I was on a roll, closing in on the lead. But at the 7th hole Butch Baird, my playing partner, hit his drive to within about a foot of the same earth crack.

"Wow, I got lucky," Baird said. "If I had gone into that crack, it would have cost me a shot."

"What do you mean, it would have cost you a shot?" I said. "You get a free drop from there."

"No, you don't," Baird said. "They didn't put it on the rules sheet."

A rules official drove by in his cart a few minutes later. He confirmed what Baird told me.

"We forgot to put it on the rules sheet," the official said.

I knew right then exactly what I needed to do. I picked up my ball and walked off the course.

"What the hell are you doing?" the official said.

"I knocked it in the earth crack on Thursday," I responded. "Demaret said I could take a drop, which I did. That means I signed an incorrect scorecard. I have to disqualify myself."

"That's goofy," the official said. "Who cares? Just keep playing, and we'll discuss the matter when we get in."

Who cares? Just keep playing?

I couldn't believe what I was hearing. From a rules official, no less.

There was nothing to discuss. I knew I was wrong, and that's all that counted.

I packed up my belongings and left the grounds without the press finding out. In hindsight my mistake was not tracking down an official before taking Demaret's word. There were probably only two or three on the whole course, but that was no excuse. I should have waited. In any case, I learned my lesson. Never again did I leave the first tee without a rules sheet in my pocket or depend on my playing partners for a ruling.

The incident in San Antonio reminded me of an earlier episode in New Orleans. I was playing with Al Besselink, one of the tour's all-time characters, and Fred Hawkins. On the par-5 5th hole, our second shots finished very close to each other. We were all playing the U.S. Royal ball, though with different numbers. I was first to play. Once on the green, Hawkins was preparing to mark his ball when he noticed a problem.

"You and I hit the wrong ball," he told Besselink.

"Keep it down, keep it quiet," Besselink said.

"What do you mean, keep it quiet?" Hawkins said.

"Just play the damn thing," Besselink continued. "No one is going to know what happened. Who is going to know?"

"Venturi, who is standing right over there," Hawkins replied.

"He don't give a shit about us," Besselink said. "He's going to beat us anyway."

Hawkins was not swayed. He picked up his ball, and both players were assessed two-stroke penalties. Besselink was flabbergasted.

"Can you believe that dumb son of a bitch?" he said to me.

"No, I can't, Bessie," I said and then cracked up. I can't really fault Bessie. I knew he was only kidding. Both balls, after all, were in almost the exact same place. But rules were rules.

Some things weren't so amusing, however, such as the practice of split purses and appearance fees, both of which I strongly opposed.

The idea of splitting purses was brought up when two players tied after 72 holes. The proposal would never come from a player, of course; nobody would risk the appearance of being intimidated by a fellow competitor. That news would get around our tiny, insular golf community in no time. Instead, a third party, perhaps a mutual friend, would ask if each combatant would agree to split the sum of first and second-place earnings.

For instance, if first prize was $3,500 and second $2,000, the playoff winner would write a check to the loser for the difference, which, in this case, would be $750. Such an arrangement would eliminate any pressure, guaranteeing both players a healthy paycheck. I didn't believe in split purses, and not just because it was unfair to the spectators who paid good money to watch a duel between players trying their best. I didn't believe in it because, despite my poor record in playoffs, I felt good about my chances against anybody. Yet, on occasion, the practice of split purses did go on.

So, unfortunately, did the acceptance of appearance fees, which disturbed me even more. I was on the committee that voted to get it banned, but tournament officials often found a back door by offering players money to speak at a luncheon or do an outing; in effect, these were still appearance fees. I understood why the players went for it—making the cut in our day did not mean making a check. Roughly half of the remaining field didn't take home any cash. (I still oppose the practice, though. When a prominent player receives a lot of money to play overseas, that tournament's credibility is seriously damaged. Golfers should be paid depending on *how* they play, not *whether* they play. And what about the other players in the field? How would they feel?)

After San Antonio, I faced another major disappointment—failing to qualify for the 1961 U.S. Open. This was the tournament I expected to win someday, the one I had fantasized about in my private commentaries at Harding Park. Now, for the first time since 1955, I would not even be in the field.

A few months later I was in the car accident in Cleveland that injured my back and ribs. In retrospect it's easy to say that I should have taken time off to properly heal. If a player today were to suffer similar injuries, he would be more cautious and would likely not return to the tour for weeks, maybe months. In the meantime, he wouldn't have to worry about making money.

Despite the lingering pain, I was able to string together a few decent performances in 1961. I wound up 14th on the money list, with $25,572, but I was way behind Gary Player, who finished on top with $64,540.

A few months later, at least, there was one factor in my favor—it was a new year. Golfers think a lot like die-hard baseball fans: hope springs eternal.

For me, a tie for fourth at the Crosby was a sign that this year would be different. My amateur partner that week was the popular entertainer Dean Martin, who could play well. We were in an excellent position to win the team competition until Sunday arrived. No, it wasn't an opponent who knocked us out; it was Mother Nature. The final round would be postponed until Monday due to snow. "I've got to go," Martin said when I met him in his room. "I'm making a movie, and I've got a contract. I've got to be in Los Angeles on Monday."

"Dean," I pleaded, "you can make a movie anytime you want. We're going to win the Crosby. You'll probably never have a chance like this again in your life." My plea did not work. Martin went to do his movie. Some 30 years later, not long before he passed away, I ran into him at his favorite Italian restaurant in Los Angeles. He was known for dining alone, but on this occasion he asked me to join him. "You know, the worst thing that ever happened to me was when I left you at Pebble Beach," he said. I knew he was exaggerating, but I still appreciated the gesture.

Two weeks after the Crosby, I teed it up in Palm Springs. For the second year in a row, the week ended in misery. This time the consequences would be far more severe. I was picking the ball out of the hole when I felt pains in my chest. I staggered through the rest of the fourth round, even posting a 68, but when I woke up the next morning, the pain was too severe for me to play the fifth, and final, round. The next few weeks were horrible. For the first time, I was scared that my career could be over. I didn't know what to do.

Slowly my health improved, although by then my swing, which I had altered to compensate for the discomfort, was a total mess—short, fast, and flat. One player after another asked if something was wrong. Nothing, I insisted, mindful always of what my father told me: never make excuses. Did I want to share my secret with my colleagues? Did I want them to know this wasn't the real Ken Venturi, that I was operating at 40, maybe 50, percent? Absolutely, but I wasn't going to be the one to tell them.

Instead, I lied. I told them I was experimenting with new swing theories. "I'm just going through a bad stretch," I said. "I'll be OK." I spent many evenings on the road alone, in my hotel room, which was nothing new. I had spent my adolescence alone.

Why didn't I call Byron Nelson? Good question, and I don't have a good answer. I imagine it was because I was too proud or too stupid. I felt he had already done so much for me, and that it wouldn't be fair to ask the man to do any more. Besides, I was determined to fix this problem on my own, just as I coped with my speech difficulties. Nelson was hurt, I was told, that I didn't call him, and I couldn't blame him. Even Lowery was turned off by my aloofness. "Kenny, have you got a dictionary at your house?" Lowery said. "Go home and look up the word *humble*— h-u-m-b-l-e."

Lowery was wrong about one thing, though. He told the press that one of my problems was that I was trying too hard to out-drive Palmer. That was total nonsense. I already could drive it as far as Palmer, if necessary. When he and I played exhibitions, I could, at times, blow it right by him. There were a lot of lies being told. I didn't have the time or the energy to deal with all of them, and it probably wouldn't have made any difference.

In April, after two months off, I finally returned to action and tied for ninth at The Masters. I was rusty, but I had every reason to think that, despite my horrible luck, I could still put together a good year. But then came the tour's Texas swing, and I had every reason to think differently. First, I finished 41st at the Texas Open. Two weeks later I reached another new low, unfortunately, at the Colonial, the home of Ben Hogan.

I shot an 80 in the first round. I was in so much pain, physical and mental, that I knew I had to get out of there fast. Of course, I couldn't just quit in the middle of a round. That wasn't my style. Instead, I reversed my score on the last two holes, deliberately signing an incorrect scorecard to get disqualified. It was stupid, I remarked at the time. But hey, looking stupid was sure a lot better than looking pathetic. I'm not proud of what I did, but I know why I did it. I had fallen so far, so fast.

The rest of the season went much the same way, filled with one mediocre performance after another. I failed again to qualify for the Open, and then about a month later went through an experience at the Canadian Open that brought even more anguish, even though it had nothing to do with my game.

I was paired with Gary Player and Art Wall Jr. at Laval sur le Lac in Quebec. On the 10th hole, Player hit his ball into the trees under some branches and was forced to punch out. After he finished the hole, I asked him for his score.

"Six," he said.

"OK," I said, marking it down.

Two holes later, a friend asked me what Player scored at the 10th hole. I said six. He told me that Player had actually recorded a seven, that he whiffed on his first attempt to dislodge the ball from under the trees. I decided to ask Player again.

"Is six what you had at No. 10?" I said.

"Yes," Player said.

As far as I was concerned, the matter was over. I wasn't about to doubt the integrity of Gary Player. Besides, I didn't see a thing. I signed my card and started the long walk to the clubhouse. I turned around at one point and saw that Player was still sitting at the scorer's table. Nonetheless, I didn't think much of it.

That evening, while I was in the middle of dinner with Bo Wininger, the phone rang.

"Hello, Ken, this is Gary. You've made a terrible mistake," Player said. "On No. 10, you put me down for a six. I had a seven."

"You said six. I showed you the card," I said, knowing that if there had been any terrible mistake, Player had been the one to make it.

"But you didn't understand," he went on. "I had a six with fresh air."

"Fresh air, fresh anything, fresh my ass," I said. "I showed you the card, and it was a six."

Player, who had won the PGA Championship a week earlier, told me that he had disqualified himself, but I, typically, was the one who took the brunt of criticism from the press. The headlines the next day made me out as the biggest criminal since Al Capone:

Venturi can't play golf anymore. He can't keep score. He gets the PGA Champion disqualified.

When I arrived at the course the following day, I was greeted by the kind of boos I hadn't received since Augusta in the late fifties. People claimed that I, too, should be disqualified for not keeping Player's correct score. I was furious, determined to go to the press and tell the truth. This kind of scenario, like the ruling with Palmer at the 1958 Masters, wouldn't happen on today's tour. There are too many people around. But back then, golf operated under the radar.

Once again, I kept my mouth shut. One of the tour's PR guys pleaded with me that going public would damage the tour. To this day, I regret that I listened to him. Weeks later, I ran into Gary Player at another tournament. I was still upset.

"You weren't truthful with me," I said. "You really embarrassed me."

"You didn't understand," he said.

"Bullshit," I told him.

I respect Gary Player for the record he compiled and for the courageous stand he took on racial equality in his native South Africa. Many high-profile players in his position would have been satisfied with the status quo, but he was not. Yet I will always believe that he acted improperly on that day in Canada. Years later, a Canadian writer finally told the whole story, which cleared my name, but it was too late.

Mercifully the 1962 season came to a close. In 19 events, I earned only $6,951 (66th on the money list), finishing with just two top 10s, none since The Masters in April. Compared to Arnold Palmer's excellence, the emergence of rookie Jack Nicklaus (who captured the U.S. Open in Palmer's backyard, Oakmont Country Club), and Billy Casper's outstanding play, I was no longer considered part of the game's upper echelon. Little did I realize that, as bad as things were, they were about to get worse.

At home Conni and I had drifted farther apart than ever. My success on the course had kept us together for the past few years. With the steep decline in my play—and subsequent decline in our bank account—I was no longer such a prize catch. The tensions between us, always so dangerously close to the surface, began to crop up with alarming frequency.

In one especially ugly exchange, she told me that she wasn't used to settling for this kind of lifestyle. We tried to keep Matt, who was six, and Tim, three, away from our line of fire, but they surely knew something was very wrong. A house is a small place when there is a war going on.

Going back on the road, for all its troubles, at least provided an escape from the turmoil in Hillsborough, or so I thought. I started out the 1963 campaign with the same familiar mediocrity—30th in

Los Angeles, 53rd at the Crosby. If that wasn't discouraging enough, it soon became evident that there would be fewer opportunities for me to make a better impression. I was also no longer a prize catch for the tournament directors, who stopped inviting me. I suppose I could have become one of the tour's "rabbits," by earning a spot through Monday qualifying. But once again, my pride got in the way. I had won 10 tournaments. Let them come to me. They didn't.

Over the next few months, one disappointment was followed by the next. I finished 34th at Augusta—no rounds in the 60s—and failed, for the third year in a row, to qualify for the U.S. Open. I gave serious thought to quitting the game, but it was my dad who put that thought out of my mind, at least for a while. "It will work out," he said. "Just believe in it and don't give up." Yet, when it became clear to me that it was most definitely *not* working out, I turned elsewhere to express my frustrations.

One escape was the track. No, I didn't bet on the horses; I drove the cars. I became enthralled by the sheer thrill of hitting those corners at very high speeds. What I didn't realize at the time was that racing represented the part of me that was looking for a way to escape all the misery. A sane person wouldn't have tried it. Of course, I wasn't sane.

Another escape was the bottle. I always enjoyed a few cocktails or beers with the boys, but my drinking went from casual to, well, chronic. Which is how, on that September afternoon in 1963, I found myself with a Jack Daniels in my hand at the bar in San Francisco.

I had nowhere else to go.

Chapter Eleven

STARTING OVER

The lecture I received from Dave Marcelli at the bar in San Francisco was only the beginning. For what he said to truly make any difference, I needed to follow up, and not just on the range at California Golf Club. That was the easy part. I had loved hitting balls ever since my teenage days at Harding Park, my haven from humiliation. The harder part was mental. I needed to stop feeling sorry for myself, to stop trying to understand why I wasn't the new Ben Hogan. I needed to look ahead, not behind. Ben Hogan didn't win his first major until he was 34 years old. I was only 32.

My performance at the Sahara Invitational in Las Vegas was the first encouraging sign in a long time, even if I struggled on the final day with a 76. With three rounds of 70 or better, I proved, once again, that I could compete against the best players in the world. During my other appearances on the tour in 1963—I finished 94th on the money list—that hadn't been the case. I finally had some momentum heading into 1964.

I also had some apprehension. I knew it was a do-or-die year for me. I wasn't as fortunate as today's players, who can better endure prolonged slumps. For one thing, many have long-term equipment deals or other lucrative endorsements, paying as much as six figures per year. Practically every part of their bodies is sold to the highest bidder. For another, even the players who end up far back on the official money list do exceptionally well. Carlos Franco, who finished 94th in 2003, the same position I placed in 1963, earned $672,022. If that constitutes a slump, sign me up.

I was going broke and the only outside income keeping me and my family afloat—contracts with U.S. Royal and Jantzen, a shirt and sweater manufacturing company—would soon be running out. It didn't take a marketing genius to realize that they would look elsewhere if I continued my mediocre play. Crunching the numbers in my bank account, I figured there was just enough for one final push. Once the money ran out, as I vowed in 1957, I would return to San Francisco to sell cars.

The season kicked off at Rancho Park in Los Angeles, a place where I had won before. Why not make it a place, I thought to myself, where I could win again? Swinging without pain and incorporating the lessons I picked up from Byron Nelson, I was ready but missed the cut. I played well enough, but couldn't score, which is an entirely different skill from hitting the ball. The drive back to San Francisco was long, with a lot of soul searching. All my work at California Golf Club seemed like a huge waste of time.

When I arrived home I went to see Bill Varni, a close friend, who owned the Owl and Turtle Restaurant in downtown San Francisco. I was in bad shape.

"Bill, I just don't know if I can make it," I said. "I thought I was close, but it's just not happening."

Varni was like my dad, a master motivator. He knew precisely what to say.

"Ken, I'll tell you what I'll do," he said, reaching for his checkbook. "I'll give you $50,000 right now, but you've got to give me everything you win this coming year and everything you endorse after you win this year."

He started writing the check.

"Are you crazy?" I told him. "I know what you're trying to do. You're trying to screw me out of all my winnings. Keep the money. I'm going to do it on my own!"

I came across as pretty adamant, but the truth was the exact opposite. If anybody other than Bill Varni had made that kind of offer, I probably would've taken it. I sure needed the 50 grand. But I didn't want to take advantage of him.

He offered me a beer. "No thanks," I said. "I've got things I have to do."

I went back to California Golf Club, the words from Hogan playing over and over in my head: "Every day you miss practicing will take you one day longer to be good. . . . There isn't enough daylight in any one day to practice all the shots you need to."

I worked harder on my short game. The best tempo I ever developed came from hitting bunker shots. I also started to swing more slowly to keep myself in a smooth rhythm. The results, however, did not come fast enough. The doubts would not go away: could I ever really be the player I was once before?

I missed another cut, at the Crosby, with my friends, family, and Byron Nelson in attendance. I came up short in Palm Springs and finished 39th in the Lucky International in San Francisco, earning just $95. Turning down Bill Varni's 50 grand looked more questionable with each passing week. I would be fortunate to make 20 grand for the whole year.

But all was not lost. During the San Francisco tournament, I became better acquainted with a local pastor, Father Francis Kevin Murray, whom I had met briefly the year before. Father Murray, who could see the trouble I was in, soon began to come around the house. We played a little golf and went for long walks, talking about trust, confidence, dedication . . . about life. He showed tremendous faith in me, which helped me to have more faith in myself. I learned how to become a better man, how to develop true compassion for myself and for others. In his own way, he taught me as much as Byron Nelson had. Nelson worked on my swing. Father Murray worked on my inner self.

His guidance couldn't have come at a more opportune time. The Masters was around the corner, the perfect arena for me to stage my comeback. I usually played well at Augusta National, even during my slump. Imagine if, after the setbacks in 1956, 1958, and 1960 and my recent struggles, I were to finally win the green jacket. It would certainly have the makings of a Hollywood screenplay. I began to perform much better—a tie for 9th in Pensacola (my first four-figure check in two years) and a tie for 15th at Doral. The plot was thickening.

But there would be no Hollywood screenplay, not in April. Someone changed the script. After my loss in 1960, Cliff Roberts assured me: "You will always be invited back to Augusta." Thus, for weeks when Conni told me the invitation hadn't arrived yet, I was not overly concerned. I was sure it would come any day. Roberts would keep his word. But, as the days wore on, the invitation did not come. It never came. For the first time since 1955, I would not be going to The Masters. I had been through a lot of lows in the past three years, but this was a new one. The greatest players in the game would meet on the greatest stage, and I was left out.

I was immediately faced with two choices: go back to self-pity —and perhaps the bottle—or be more resolved than ever to reclaim my rightful spot in the game I treasured. I chose the latter. Nothing ever inspires me as much as when people count me out, and I never felt as counted out as I did in April of 1964. I went through bag after bag at California Golf Club, probably hitting more balls in one week than in any week ever. I didn't watch one second of the tournament, staying outside until I was sure the telecast was over. To this day, I can't provide any details of what happened. (Arnold Palmer, the record indicates, became the first player to win four Masters, coasting by six shots over Jack Nicklaus and Dave Marr.) I'll be back in 1965, I promised myself.

Inspired or not, I still couldn't make any top 10s. I was picking up a little change here and there, including about $1,500 on the Texas swing, but my financial outlook was still precarious. I wasn't going to borrow any money, either. I was going to make it on my own or fail on my own. Some people suspected that I might resort to desperate measures. But I was a lot tougher than that.

Prayer was a different matter. One night, in May, I was at my workbench in the basement polishing my clubs, a routine I started as a teenager. My clubs were my tools, priceless objects that required special care. I fetched a bucket of water and soap and cleanser, and cleaned every iron carefully: the shafts, the heads, the grips, everything. I was alone with my clubs and my thoughts in the same safe world I had built for myself so many years before, the one world the bullies could never enter.

I don't recall the presence of any overhead lights, only a small lamp turned down very low. Suddenly, my thoughts took on a new sense of urgency. Looking at my clubs, I put my arms on the bench, kneeled down, and blessed myself.

"Lord, please don't let me die like this," I whispered. "I don't know the reason why all of this has happened to me, but please put the clubs back in my hands just one more time. I promise I will find a way to give back. Do with me what you will, but please give me one more chance."

I don't know how long I prayed. Hours, perhaps, until 3:00 or 4:00 in the morning. All I know for sure is that when I went down to the garage the following afternoon, the clubs were nice and clean, in their proper place in the bag, and my mind, too, was in its proper place. I was ready to make the most of that one last chance.

Praying alone wouldn't do it. I needed to putt better. Enter Bud Ward and the answer from a most unlikely source. Shortly before I headed off to tournaments in Oklahoma and Tennessee, Ward, a longtime friend in San Francisco and winner of the 1939 and 1941 U.S. Amateurs, handed me a rare Ben Hogan pacemaker MacGregor center shaft putter from his closet. The putter featured a leather grip, with the initials P. J. G. stamped on the bottom. The putter came with a story.

For many years, it had belonged to Phil Garnett, a sweet, kind, slightly hunchback man who was a member of California Golf Club. Shortly before he passed away, Garnett gave his putter to Ward. "Bud," he said, "someday you will find someone who really needs this putter. You give it to him and you tell him it will work."

I took it to the putting green right away. Golfers will try anything once. "Well, Philly," I said, "let me see how good you are, pal."

Philly was really good. I started rolling them in one after another from everywhere. Philly, I decided right then, would be joining me on the road.

Philly could only do so much. The rest was up to me, which was why I did no better than 27th in Oklahoma and 28th in Tennessee. I did, however, pass one very crucial test: firing rounds of 67 and 70 at Memphis Country Club to get through the first stage of U.S. Open qualifying. I hadn't competed in the Open, which would be played at Congressional Country Club in Washington, D.C., since 1960, and now I was halfway there. Sectional qualifying was a few weeks away.

In the minds of many in the golf community, I was still nowhere. Which is why it wasn't a complete shock when I received the call from Janzten, which also employed star athletes Bob Cousy, Paul Hornung, and Frank Gifford.

"When are we going to do the next shoot?" I asked.

"We've already done the shoot," a company spokesman said. "We got somebody else. We're going to let you go. We feel that your game is over the hill (the same words Conni used). We need someone with a fresher, brighter name." Apparently, sensitivity was not this guy's strong suit.

The fresher, brighter name, it turned out, was Dave Marr, who would win the 1965 PGA Championship and become a well-respected television commentator. Marr had no trouble stepping in even before I was officially fired, which I never forgot. I also could never forget what Jantzen did. I understood their reasoning. The bottom line was, well, the bottom line. Even so, they should've told me that I was being let go *before* they hired Marr. They owed me that, if nothing else. As usual, I used the situation to my advantage, as another slight to motivate me. I stopped racing cars, as well.

Now that I was playing better, I sure wasn't going to blow it by doing something stupid.

After Tennessee, I headed to the tournament in Indianapolis. I wanted to play well, no doubt, but I was also thinking ahead. If I could make the cut, I would gain automatic entry into the Thunderbird Classic a week later at the Westchester Country Club just outside New York City. The Thunderbird offered a $100,000 purse, an opportunity I couldn't let slip by. There weren't too many left.

Maybe I thought too far ahead. I missed the cut in Indy by one stroke when someone chipped in on the last hole. One stroke or a million strokes, it made no difference. I wasn't going to New York. I was, it seemed increasingly clear, going nowhere. I stayed in town over the weekend to watch a good friend, Johnny Boyd, compete in the Indianapolis 500. At least one of us was in a position to win something.

I had asked God for one more chance and nothing happened. It was time to ask Bill Jennings. To me, in May of 1964, Jennings was almost as important. My money was nearly gone. Jennings, owner of the New York Rangers, was also Thunderbird's tournament director. After missing the cut at Indianapolis, I called him to see if there was any hope of landing a sponsor's exemption. The one thing going for me was my name, which still counted for something. But there was one thing going against me, and I figured I might as well put it out in the open.

"Mr. Jennings, if you don't give me an invite, I can't condemn you," I said. "I made an ass of myself by shooting 80 last year and withdrawing. I embarrassed myself and I embarrassed the tournament. I'm so close to playing well, to winning, but I don't have the money. If I don't get the invite, I'm going back to selling cars. My career will be over."

"We only have one invitation left," Jennings said. "Call me back tomorrow and I'll let you know."

There was nothing more for me to do. The next day, I hung out with Johnny Boyd's crew in the pits. He ran a fantastic race, finishing fifth behind A. J. Foyt Jr. As I congratulated Boyd, all he wanted to know was whether I received the invite. Believe it or not, I had forgotten all about it. I was more worried about my good friend and, I suppose, afraid of getting another rejection and what it would signify for the rest of my career.

I called Jennings, more nervous than I had been in a long time. He then said the five words that would change my life:

"Yes, you've got the invite."

I told Johnny Boyd, who was very excited. Too excited, in fact.

"My race is over," he said, "but my good friend, Ken Venturi, is going to New York [for the Thunderbird] and is going to win the U.S. Open."

He obviously was spending way too much time behind the wheel.

"Are you crazy?" I said.

"No," Boyd said, "I believe it."

There was no point in discussing the matter any further. I was headed to New York.

Boyd wasn't the only one who believed in me. So did another friend, well-known restaurant owner Toots Shor. Shor's establishment in the sixties was the in-place in the Big Apple, always filled with athletes and movie stars. On the Tuesday of the Thunderbird week, Shor asked me to come for dinner, sending a limo to pick me up. There was no bill that night, and when I tried to tip the waiter, he told me he would be fired if he accepted a single cent. I was quite moved. Here I was, my career on the ropes, and yet I was receiving star treatment from Toots Shor.

"Toots," I said, "I can't thank you enough. I promise when I make it, I'll be back."

"I know you will," he told me, putting me in the limo. "Good luck."

At Westchester, I got off to a fabulous start, shooting a 67 on one of the tour's most demanding layouts. I followed with rounds of 70 and 72. Midway through the final round, I realized I had a chance to win the tournament. But when I arrived at the 16th, a difficult par-3 with water on the left and sand on the right surrounding a narrow green, I was thinking about protecting, not advancing, my position. I was worried about losing money.

I figured I would lay up with a 4 iron, taking the bunkers out of play. A chip and a putt, and I'd have my three, four at the worst. If I went for the pin, five would enter the equation. With a bogey, and pars at the last two holes, even if I didn't win, I would still pick up a substantial check.

But, suddenly, looking at the green for what seemed like a lifetime, a different thought entered my mind with surprising, almost alarming, force. I said to myself: "If you back off now, you will back off for the rest of your life." I went for the pin, knocking a 3 iron to within 15 feet, 2-putting for par. Even after a birdie at 17 and a par at 18, I tied for third, three strokes behind Tony Lema, and two behind Mike Souchak. No matter. I didn't back off and I would never back off again.

I signed my card and went directly to the back of the locker room. I sat there for the longest time, bawling my eyes out. I had arrived in New York broke and desperate, a missed cut or two away from the end. Now, with $6,250 in my pocket, there was hope at last. I tracked down Bill Jennings in the clubhouse. What do you say to the man who has saved your life? Thank you, I suppose, as if that could ever be enough. Nothing could ever be enough.

My third-place finish also qualified me for the following week's tournament, the Buick Open Invitational in Grand Blanc, Michigan, where I tied for sixth, earning another $2,344. On the way, I stopped in nearby Detroit, at Franklin Hills, for the last stage of U.S. Open qualifying. I was playing well at the perfect time.

At least I thought I was playing well. With a horrific 77 in the morning round, it appeared inevitable that I would miss the Open for the fourth year in a row. Other players who recorded a similar score didn't even bother to show up for the afternoon round. Not me, not if I ever wanted to face my dad again. On the first hole of the second 18, against a stiff wind, I hit a driver and a 1 iron to within two feet and converted the putt. I went on to shoot 70, qualifying by two strokes. I was able to get through both local and sectional qualifying in the same year.

I was back in the Open.

Chapter Twelve

REDEMPTION

I arrived in Washington, D.C., on Monday. Being gone for four long years made me appreciate every moment of U.S. Open week. Like many blessed to be a professional golfer, I didn't completely realize my good fortune until it was taken away. I wasn't going to make the same mistake again.

My top priority the first few days was getting to know the golf course better. Congressional, in my initial assessment, seemed to be the perfect setup for my game. At 7,053 yards, the longest course in U.S. Open history, it would require excellent long iron play, which was my forte. Nonetheless, I needed to absorb as much as possible about Congressional's subtleties, about where I should try to hit it, and, just as important, where it was safe to miss it. How much knowledge I picked up would depend heavily on my caddie, which is where I received my first big break of the week.

In 1964 a tour player wasn't allowed to bring his regular caddie to the U.S. Open. Instead I picked a name out of a hat from a list provided by the host club. The name I picked was William

Ward, who just happened to be the course's highest-rated caddie. I was delighted, although William, I could only imagine, didn't feel quite the same way. William had a lot of kids to feed. Drawing Arnold Palmer or Jack Nicklaus, who would offer the likelihood of a more lucrative payday, is closer to what I'm sure he had in mind.

"William, I know you're not too happy about having me, but I think I can win this tournament," I said.

William could tell I was serious.

"I'll do the best for you, Mr. Ken," he said.

"We'll give it a good, hard try."

On Tuesday morning I played a nine-hole practice round with Paul Harney, who was surprised to see me.

"Aren't you going to the White House?" he asked.

I didn't have a clue of what he was talking about. The White House, he told me, was hosting a lawn party for the favorites, the leading contenders, and the past champions. I didn't have a clue because I wasn't invited. No problem. I used the rejection as a motivating factor. Thank you, President Johnson.

"It's more important for me to get in a practice round," I told Harney.

Another 9 holes with Paul Harney on Wednesday—it was too hot to play 18—provided me with additional insight. I was as ready as I would ever be.

Finally, play began. Paired with Billy Maxwell and George Bayer, the U.S. Open pressure got to me, simple as that. I considered myself one of the game's finest bunker players, but on the front nine I failed *twice* to get the ball out on my first try. Fortunately, with my second try, I got up and down each time to save bogey. Doubles would have been disastrous. I was 3 over at the turn, with the tougher nine yet to go. But demonstrating the kind of grit that was missing from my game for so long, I scrambled for a 2-over 72. I was four shots behind Palmer, but at least I could see him.

My second round was a marked improvement. All aspects of my game were working. Except for the first hole, I drove it without using a tee. I kicked up the turf, hitting sliders off the ground that, essentially, helped me eliminate the left side of the course. My approaches found the right spots on the greens, and I made my share of crucial putts. Throughout my slump, all I wanted to do was get the ball close enough for a par. Now I was thinking birdie.

So was my good friend Tommy Jacobs, who shot a remarkable, record-tying 64, highlighted by a 60-foot putt on 18. Palmer, after a 69, was within one. After an even-par 70, I was six back. In the old days, I would have been very disappointed to face such a large deficit at the halfway mark. But these were new days, difficult days, days of lower expectations. I had told my caddie I could win, but winning wasn't really on my mind. I came to Congressional to make a strong showing, to qualify for a return to Augusta and perhaps the 1965 Open. So far, so good.

Over the next 24 hours everything changed. Forever.

It started with a letter I found in my locker. The letter, six pages long, came from Father Murray. I read it in the car on my way to the hotel. I read it over and over and over:

> *If you would win the U.S. Open, you would prove to millions of people that they can be victorious over doubt and struggle and temptation to despair. . . . Your success would be*

a world of encouragement to everyone. . . . You have always had the ability, and since the beginning of the year this ability has been getting sharper and steadier. . . . You want it for your own satisfaction, after suffering humiliation and frustration in the past . . . to show the world that you are made of championship caliber. . . . You are truly the new Ken Venturi . . . now wise and mature and battle-toughened.

Father Murray went on to make specific suggestions:

- *Keep your mood from getting emotionally disturbed from elation or disappointment.*
- *Make the clear determination and make the act of your will to follow that definite plan of action.*
- *Give yourself over entirely to the fulfillment of your one shot at hand.*
- *Trust in your swing and in your ability.*
- *Get the birdies during the early holes. When you see you are in contention it will give you more spirit and inspiration to fight consistently and bravely and hopefully.*

Father Murray demonstrated a surprisingly acute knowledge of the game, advising me to practice with only one ball on the putting green, not two or three, which was my routine. "The reason for this," he wrote, "is to simulate playing conditions where you only have one putt at the hole. Also it forces a man to concentrate solely on the one practice putt."

His advice made so much sense. Suddenly, I felt a kind of peace I had never felt before. I decided to go to church that evening. Praying in a hotel room wouldn't do.

I found a Catholic church close to the hotel, but it was locked. Fortunately the priest was gracious enough to open the doors. I stayed for nearly an hour, going back and forth between reading Father Murray's letter and reciting my own personal prayers. I didn't ask God for a victory. God doesn't care who wins the U.S. Open. "Please let me believe in myself," I said. "I know that my faults are many, but please let me play well and comport myself like a man, no matter what happens."

I walked outside and thanked the priest. "Good luck, tomorrow," he said.

Back at my hotel, I found more inspiration. I watched *Champion*, a film starring Kirk Douglas as a boxer who refused to surrender. He kept getting himself up off the mat, which was exactly what I was trying to do.

When I woke up Saturday morning, the peace I felt was even more profound. I was about to tee it up on the final day of the game's most prestigious championship, and I was as relaxed as if I were getting ready for a practice round at Harding Park. Tony Lema, one of my best friends on tour, noticed the change in me right away. "You look great today, Ken," he said on the putting green. "You know something, I have a feeling it's going to be your day."

"I sure hope so, Tony," I said.

I kept putting, practicing with only one ball, as Father Murray suggested. If he ever got tired of the priesthood, it occurred to me, he might have a future in the golf business.

The final day of the U.S. Open is always the game's most exacting test, 36 holes of trying to negotiate narrow fairways, deep rough, fast greens, and fragile emotions. On every hole, par, as the cliché goes, is a good score. This year's contest would be even tougher than usual. No fault, to be fair, of the USGA. The blame belonged to Mother Nature. It was hot, really hot, and it would get even hotter. Today was going to be a challenge just to survive.

My playing partner was Ray Floyd, a promising 21-year-old kid. I remembered when I was a promising 21-year-old kid—a lifetime ago.

On the opening hole, I received a sign that maybe Tony Lema was right. Maybe today was going to be my day. I sent my approach on the par-4 to about 12 feet and hit what I thought was a wonderful putt. But the ball stopped on the lip, refusing to take one more small dive into the hole. I stared at it for as long as I could under the rules, hoping to will the ball into the cup. I gave up, finally, and walked over to tap it in. At that moment, the ball disappeared. A gift, I decided, freeing me to toss aside my conservative game plan. "You have one shot to play with," I told myself. "Fire at every flag until you lose that shot."

Making that putt also made an impression on a certain spectator in the gallery, Vince Lombardi. Lombardi, the legendary coach of the Green Bay Packers, told a friend that he was convinced I would be the champion.

"How can you tell?" the friend asked.

"Just take a look at him," Lombardi said. "His eyes are dead. They're the coldest I've ever seen. He beats them going away." (Over the years, a few of his players told me that Lombardi often brought my name up during his halftime speeches to motivate them. "You look into that guy across from you on the line," he would say, "and his eyes better know that your eyes own him. The greatest eyes I ever saw in my life were Ken Venturi's when he stared at that ball. I feel he made the ball move." Last time I saw

Lombardi, about four years later, he was still talking about it. "I'll never forget that look on your face," he said.)

The change in strategy kept paying off. My card for the front nine was one to be framed: 3-3-4, 3-3-4, 3-3-4, a total of 5-under 30. I was getting my birdies early, just like Father Murray advised. Given the circumstances, it has to be, without a doubt, the finest nine holes of golf I've ever played. More importantly, with Palmer struggling and Jacobs cooling off a bit, I was right back in the tournament. I picked up another birdie on 12 to go 6 under for the day. Six more pars and I would match Tommy Jacobs with my own 64.

But I would not finish with a 64, or, for that matter, a 65. I would, in fact, be fortunate to finish at all.

The heat—the temperature had risen to near 100 degrees—was getting to me. I wasn't used to this kind of weather. I was a product of the Bay Area, familiar with fog and rain and mist—you know, Crosby weather.

After making pars at 15 and 16, I hit my approach at 17 to within about 15 feet. I missed the putt, leaving me about a foot and a half for par. But as I lined it up, my whole body began to shake. I thought I was going to faint. I pulled the putter back but had no idea where it was going. I missed, needless to say, notching my first bogey of the day. At 18, after being short of the green, I chipped to about three feet. Again I was shaking and could hardly see the hole, resulting in another bogey; 64 had quickly turned into 66.

My score was the least of my problems. There were still another 18 holes to play, and it wasn't going to get any cooler.

I dropped the putter and staggered to a station wagon for the drive up the hill to the clubhouse. From then on, except for a few brief moments, I can't remember a single thing that happened until I reached the 16th hole about four hours later. All I can do is go by what others have told me. Following is their account:

I joined Jay Hebert in the front seat. "Think you can make it back to the clubhouse?" Hebert asked me. "Your eyes are rolling in your head." I did make it to the clubhouse, where I was promptly greeted by Dr. John Everett, a Congressional member and chairman of the Open's medical committee. Dr. Everett was asked to check me out. What he found was not good. I was suffering from heat prostration. Despite the unbearable conditions, I didn't drink any water during my round or take any salt tablets. The only salt I knew about was the kind they put on eggs. Pretty naive, huh? I guess so. I suppose the only explanation is that I was so focused on the task at hand.

Dr. Everett stretched me out on the floor next to my locker and gave me some salt tablets and iced tea. I was too sick to eat lunch. He then gave me something else to digest.

"If it were up to me right now, Ken, I would take you to the hospital," he said. "You can't go out there. It could be fatal."

"It's better than the way I've been living," I responded, and got off the floor.

I wasn't referring only to my golf game. I was referring to my whole life. The situation with Conni was more torturous than ever. While in San Francisco, I spent many nights during the week on a buddy's boat. A divorce was inevitable. Now, with everything that was on the line at Congressional, I had come too far to back down.

I could tell Dr. Everett was still worried. I told him that I would sign anything to absolve him of responsibility. It was not necessary, he said.

And back out there I went, into the heat, into the biggest round of my career, with nothing—and everything—to lose. My 66 had put me only two strokes behind Jacobs, who shot a 70. Palmer, with a 75, fell six back.

When I arrived at the first tee, some fans were relieved, as a rumor had spread that I wasn't going to be able to continue. Only 50 minutes had gone by since my bogey at 18. I could've used a much longer break, but it wasn't up to me. Besides, everybody else had to cope with the same time frame.

Dr. Everett went out there with me, carrying the cold towels he would put around my neck, and he had an abundant supply of salt tablets.

I split the fairway with my drive on the opening hole and went on to par the first five holes. In retrospect, being so out of sorts was a blessing. My mind was too vacant to wander to the wrong places, to the old demons. I played strictly on instinct. All I tried to do was what it always takes to win the United States Open: fairways and greens, fairways and greens. I know it's a cliché, but I was concentrating on one shot at a time, again like Father Murray suggested. I trusted my swing, unaffected by any pressure. Even a bogey at the 6th didn't throw me off my game plan. Heading to the 9th hole, I was tied with Jacobs, who doubled the second and bogeyed another hole. The game was on.

At the 9th, the 599-yard Ravine Hole, I smacked a solid drive and a good 1 iron, almost too good—the ball stopped only a few yards from the edge of the ravine. On my approach, I aimed right for the flag at the back of the green. The gamble paid off, the ball coming to a halt about nine feet from the pin. The tricky downhill putt broke right to left, caught the low side, and rolled in. I was the sole leader of the U.S. Open. Looking back at the old, grainy, black-and-white footage—boy do I wish there were VCRs in 1964—my reaction after that putt went in reveals a lot. I lifted my arm ever so slightly to celebrate and then abruptly stopped. I wish I could recall exactly what I was thinking, but I'm pretty sure I was merely following another piece of Father Murray's excellent advice: "Keep your mood from getting emotionally disturbed from elation or disappointment." There was a long way to go.

I came up with a huge save at 10, converting a short putt for par, and followed with pars at 11 and 12. I was a machine. Whenever I asked William for the yardage, he issued his standard reply. "You don't need the yardage, Mr. Ken," he said. "You're at the same exact yardage you were at in the morning." In fact, for my approaches to the green, I used the same club I did in the morning 14 times. By today's standards, I wasn't hitting it particularly long, perhaps about 250 yards, but it was good enough. More important, I was finding the fairways, and every time I faced a critical putt, I relied on Philly Garnett. "Come on Philly baby," I said, "we really need this one." Philly almost always came through.

At the 13th hole, a very exacting, 448-yard par-4, I hit one of my best drives of the day, a beautiful 6 iron to within 18 feet. I was told I took a long time to look over the putt, but I suppose it was worth the wait. When the ball fell in, I closed my eyes. There was only one person who could beat me now: me.

Which, I knew, could very well still happen, especially with the way my body was reacting to the heat. The American Red Cross reported numerous cases of heat prostration that day. One could barely breathe. On my way to losing eight pounds, I was moving slower and slower.

Too slow, I worried, which is why I approached Joe Dey, who, along with future Masters chairman Hord Hardin, was following our group.

"Joe, I'm having a hard time walking," I said. "I know that if I get too slow, I might be penalized, but let me know if I need to speed up."

"You're doing just fine," Dey said.

Soon I was on the 18th tee. For the whole round, I had purposely avoided the leader boards. There was already enough to worry about.

But after hitting my drive, it was time. I approached Bill Hoellie, a good friend whom I had known since my junior golf days in San Francisco.

"How do I stand?" I asked him.

"Just stay on your feet," Hoellie said. "We've got it."

Coming down the fairway, I finally looked at the board. My name was the only one in red, under par, which meant my lead was at least two strokes. It was, I soon found out, actually even larger. I was home free. The only way I could blow the Open was if I were to do something really stupid, such as hit my approach into the pond left of the green. Therefore, I intentionally put a slight block on the second shot with my 5 iron, steering it to the right of the green. The ball took a bad bounce off the slope and ended up in the bunker. The important thing was that I was dry.

I started my triumphant walk toward the green, doing something I had never done before the final putt dropped. I took off my white cap. "Hold your head high, Ken," Dey said, "like the champion that you are." The applause was unlike anything I ever heard. I wanted it to last forever.

Moments later, I saw something I had never seen before—two marshals rolling around in the bunker. One was working the 18th hole. The other came over from a different hole to catch all the drama. One guy kicked the other in the face. My only thought was a selfish one: don't roll on my ball! They didn't.

The bunker shot was not especially difficult. The lie was clean and there was very little lip. No problem. But, with the way I chose to execute the shot, it could have been a tremendous problem. Instead of chipping it, I did what was ingrained in me and hit the standard explosion shot, catching the sand behind the ball. Over the years, every time I watch a replay, I break into a cold sweat, aware of how easily I could have skulled it over the green into the very same water I had avoided with my approach. I could have finished with a six or seven, which would have been one of the biggest choking acts of all time.

But there would be no choking today. This was 1964, not 1956.

The ball stopped about 10 feet from the cup. I read the putt to break left to right. I pushed it about two inches too far right, but somehow it went left and fell in, only fitting that the day would end as magically as it began. I dropped my putter, and suddenly it all hit me: "My God, I've won the Open," I said. I stayed pretty composed until I looked into the eyes of Ray Floyd, who picked the ball out of the hole for me. Floyd was sobbing, and that's when I lost it.

There was one thing left to do, and it was important: sign the card. I needed to be extremely careful. One mistake and everything I worked for would mean nothing. While someone in the tent called off my scores, I started to get a little nervous, reflecting back to my good friend, Jackie Pung, the apparent winner who was disqualified in the 1957 U.S. Women's Open for signing an incorrect card. I became even more nervous when I couldn't remember if my scores were accurate. I was so out of it that when I handed Floyd his card, there wasn't one number on it. To this day, I can't tell you about a single shot he hit.

I then felt a comforting hand on my shoulder.

"Sign the card, Ken, it's correct," the voice said. I looked up, and it was Joe Dey.

After that everything happened so fast. I received congratulations from Jacobs, the man whom I had shared Christmas dinner with in Austria 10 years earlier. "Tommy, I really mean this, but if it couldn't have been me, I wish it could have been you," I said. "No," he responded. "It should have been you." I took a call from my parents, who had watched on television from California. My mom was crying so hard she could barely say a word. She was crying in victory, her son's victory. My dad, of course, the stoic one, did have something to say.

"Now you've got to prove it was no fluke," he said. Typical Dad.

"I'll show you," I told him.

Next, a U.S. Royal representative handed me a check for $10,000, the bonus the company handed out to any of their players who captured a major. I was extremely grateful. Contrary to the Jantzen company, U.S. Royal stuck by me when I went through hard times. They didn't think I was "over the hill," and, by golly, now they were being rewarded for their loyalty.

I was escorted to meet with the press, the group I hadn't been too crazy about since the unfortunate incident in 1956. We talked about Father Murray—I suggested splitting the trophy with him—the 1956 Masters, my long slump, and how I survived on this incredible day. I don't recall most of what I told them, except for a line that received a lot of play. "The last three years," I said, "when they've talked about Arnie's Army and Nicklaus' Navy, all I've had were Venturi's Vultures."

One new admirer I picked up that week was my caddie, William Ward. There is absolutely no way I would have won the Open without him. He always knew, like any good caddie, when to talk and when to be quiet. His knowledge of Congressional was invaluable. Early in the week, he took a tape measure over the course so that he could give me exact yardage. When the tournament was over, I gave him a check for $1,000. He, in turn, gave me a compliment I would cherish just as much.

"Mr. Ken, I don't mind telling you, but when you picked my name out of the hat, I wasn't too pleased," he said. "I wanted to get one of the favorites, but I want to tell you something. You're the damnedest golfer I ever saw in my life." (For several years, I spent a little time with William whenever CBS covered the Kemper tournament at Congressional. He shagged balls for me when I hit chip shots and putts for about a half hour, and I always gave him $100. The last time I saw him, he wasn't feeling too well, but he wanted to see me. I told him I wasn't in the mood to hit any balls. I hit a few putts, gave him a hug and placed in his hand two $100 bills. "Mr. Ken," he said, looking down at his hands, "it is always good to see you, and you're still the greatest.")

Finally, Conni and I left Congressional. I think we closed the place. When we arrived at our hotel, there were so many calls to return from Byron Nelson, Toots Shor, and others. I was up for hours. I was still excited from the call that came earlier in the day from Bing Crosby. "I'm so proud of you," he said. When Bing got off the line, he handed the phone to Bill Worthing, who would later be my best man when I married Beau: "I never saw him shed a tear in his life," Worthing said, "but he was sitting here crying." Another well-known entertainer was also touched by my performance—Ed Sullivan. I was booked for the following night, four months after the Beatles had made their historic appearance.

After I slept for a few hours, the phone rang again. The woman on the line was extending a very important invitation: "The president of the United States would like to have you to lunch to personally congratulate you on winning the Open," she said.

I was very excited. The White House doesn't call every day. But, believe it or not, I told her I couldn't meet President Johnson for lunch on Sunday. "No disrespect to the president," I said, "but please tell him I'm unable to make it." I had to rush to New York for the Sullivan show and lunch the following day with Toots Shor.

Before flying to New York, there was one more stop I needed to make. I went back to the same church I had attended on Friday night. So much was different now. With Mass already under way, I took a seat in the back. I didn't come to pray. I came to simply thank God for giving me a new life. "You're unbelievable," I whispered. "I don't know why you chose me, but I will never forget you for it. I promise that I will find a way to give back."

On Sunday afternoon Conni and I arrived at the studio for *The Ed Sullivan Show*, the same auditorium that David Letterman uses today. I was scared to death, to say the least. I was the one, remember, who always gave short answers, and here I was about to talk on national TV—and live, no less! I was way out of my comfort zone. Fortunately I felt much better after we rehearsed for over an hour. Sullivan, who was going to read his questions from a teleprompter, couldn't have been more accommodating. He and I had once been partners in a pro-am. This time, I was the one who needed the strokes. Finally the show started.

"Mr. Ken Venturi," Sullivan said, in that distinctive voice. "How are you doing?"

"I'm doing just fine, Ed," I said. "Thank you very much."

Live or not, this wasn't so hard. Just then, the teleprompter broke. Sullivan was at a total loss.

"So, Ken, uh, how many salt tablets did you have yesterday?" he asked. "Eighteen," I said.

That was the whole interview. There was nothing to do but go to a commercial break.

"I'm so sorry, Ken," Sullivan said.

So was I. I was on the air for less than a minute, my first experience in the pitfalls of live television. It would not be my last.

No matter. The next day I was off to the big celebration with Toots Shor. Three weeks earlier I had shown up for dinner a desperate man who almost had to beg for a sponsor's exemption. I was returning as the United States Open champion. When I arrived, the applause was overwhelming. I felt as if I were back on the 18th fairway at Congressional. Toots told me later that it was the only standing ovation he had ever seen in all of his years at the restaurant. "I knew you'd be back," he said. I was greeted by comedian Joe E. Lewis. "Vennie," Lewis said. He always called me Vennie. "I saw you win the Open. Staggering around, dropping your putter, passing out. It's the greatest act I ever saw in my life." I've borrowed that line ever since.

I received wonderful reactions the whole time I was in New York. As I walked up 52nd Street in Manhattan, motorists blew their horns at me. Cab drivers stopped right in the middle of the street and ran over to hug me or give me a kiss. Yes, New York City cab drivers! I went to another popular hangout, the "21" Club, and everyone applauded. The most amazing tribute came when I saw the Broadway hit *Hello Dolly*. The star, Carol Channing, whom I had never met before, performed a slightly different rendition: "Kenny," she sang, "it's so nice to have you back where you belong." I also attended a musical that starred Steve Lawrence and Eydie Gorme. Before their last curtain call, Lawrence addressed the audience. "We never do this," he said, "but please turn the house lights up. I want you all to meet the United States Open champion, Ken Venturi."

Carol Channing was right. It was so nice to be back where I belonged. For the longest time, I doubted I would ever belong on the tour again. Even with all the supporters—Bud Ward, Bill Varni, Father Murray—who cheered me on, and with the countless hours at California Golf Club, I was never far removed from my deepest, darkest fears: did I squander my talent forever? Would I ever make up for the way I lost the 1956 Masters?

But with the performance at Congressional—my 2-under 278 was the second-lowest score by a winner in U.S. Open history, behind Hogan's 276 in 1948—those fears were gone, presumably for good. I was ready to build on my four-shot victory and become, once again, one of the best players in the game. The future, uncertain for so long, was filled with exciting new possibilities.

At my hotel, hours after the Open victory, I did something I hadn't done in nine months. During that whole time, I had kept my promise to Dave Marcelli, the bartender from San Francisco. I wouldn't take another drink until I won again.

I had a glass of white wine.

Chapter Thirteen

BEGINNING OF THE END

Winning the Open did not change everything. It did not, for instance, change my marriage, though it did prolong it for several years. After all, how could I leave Conni now? My reputation, finally rebuilt, would come apart once again. I would be perceived as the big shot who abandoned his wife and two sons. This was the mid-sixties, before the sexual revolution, before divorce became commonplace in American society. Instead, I masqueraded as the happy husband in love with his gorgeous wife. From the looks of the photographs taken back then, I think we pulled it off, Oscars all around. But if you look closer, much closer, at some of those same pictures, it is easy to see that I was not the happy husband. I was always gazing into the distance, not at Conni. The Open was my triumph, not ours.

The children, eight and five, suffered the most. But while it greatly disturbed me, I knew I couldn't afford to think about it too much. If I did, I wouldn't be able to devote the necessary time and energy to my comeback. What I was trying to accomplish was difficult enough without tensions at home getting in the way.

On the financial front, with the $27,000 I picked up— $17,000 for the win, $10,000 from U.S. Royal—my prospects were looking a lot better. We were even able to start construction on the swimming pool that I promised Matt if I won the Open. But winning the Open did not make me rich. They say the Open is worth $1 million. Well, it wasn't worth $1 million to me, unless the argument is made that I never would have landed the lead analyst job at CBS without the credibility I had gained from winning a major. It's a good argument. Each of the analysts on the networks—Lanny Wadkins, Johnny Miller, and Curtis Strange— have won major championships.

I wasn't rich, but I was becoming more famous. On the plane ride to San Francisco a few weeks later, I was coincidentally seated next to Joe DiMaggio. I was going home to receive the key to the city and lead a parade down Market Street.

"I can't think of anything better," I told DiMaggio, "than you walking off the plane with me."

"Sure, Ken," he said. "You go on ahead, and I'll be right behind you."

But when I arrived inside the terminal, he was nowhere to be found. I later learned that he went through the catering door and escaped the whole scene. DiMaggio, always a class act, wanted me to have the stage to myself.

I signed tons of autographs in the weeks that followed the Open, and, believe me, I didn't mind for one moment. I would've signed until my hand came off. At least they were asking. They hadn't been asking for the longest time.

I was determined to do exactly what my dad suggested, to prove that the Open victory was no fluke. There were plenty of major champions who were never heard from again. I didn't want to join that club.

In July I captured the Insurance City Open Invitational in Hartford, a tournament I had been advised to skip. I was mentally and physically exhausted, but I felt a strong obligation to the officials who ran the event. Like U.S. Royal, they never stopped believing in me, extending an invite in 1963 when others were ignoring me. Anchored by a second-round 63, I prevailed by a stroke over a quartet of players including Al Besselink.

But my critics—and, yes, there were still plenty—weren't too impressed. The field, they complained, wasn't a particularly strong one. Wait until Venturi squares off against the top players on a championship-caliber course, they said. How will he do then?

Four weeks later, they found out. The site was Firestone Country Club in Akron, Ohio, the longtime home of the American Golf Classic. Except for the majors and perhaps a few other events, no event on tour attracted a more noteworthy field, which in 1964 included Palmer, Nicklaus, Player, and Lema. Furthermore, Firestone, at over 7,100 yards, was an extremely long par-70. Every part of one's game needed to be in excellent form.

In my case, every part was. After opening with a solid, 2-over 72, I shot three straight rounds in the 60s—66, 69, and 69—winning by five. I played well at the Open, obviously, but nothing like the way I performed at Firestone. I'm fairly certain that, in terms of pure ball striking, I was never more proficient, hitting long-iron approaches onto one green after another. I finished with only a few bogeys for the whole week, and that included a meaningless 3-putt at 18 on Sunday. After that performance, nobody would ever again claim the Open victory was a fluke.

That tournament also provided me with another lesson in the risks of live television. I was doing an interview with commentator Bill Flemming.

"Ken, I have never seen you so relaxed," he said. "You took your hat off. You waved to the gallery. You've always been so stern. How can you explain that?"

"Well," I told him, "it's been a great year. I won the Open and I'm going to win Player of the Year, and I broke the record here. Plus, Bill, you've got to remember: it is easy to relax when you come down the last hole with a six-shit lead."

Flemming was startled. His eyes went wide, prompting me to repeat the point.

"Bill, you've got to remember," I reiterated. "Six shots is a lot to lead by."

"You're right, Ken," he said, going quickly to a commercial.

I was reminded of that slip for years. Every time a player assumed a six-shot lead, Frank Chirkinian (CBS golf producer) would say: "You want to handle this, Venturi?"

A few weeks later, I entered the Portland Open Invitational. Although Portland was not one of the high-profile events on the tour, it carried special significance for me. The city was the home of the Jantzen Company, the people who told me I was "over the hill." I vowed to show them I wasn't. I fired three consecutive 69s and a final-round 71, but lost to a charging Jack Nicklaus on Sunday. No matter. "I would like to have won," I told the fans, "but I really wanted to show a few people here that I could still play some golf." I didn't single out the Jantzen people, but they got the message.

In my final tournament, the Almaden Open Invitational in early November, I finished fourth, my 10th top 10 finish since June. I earned $62,466 for the year, 6th on the money list.

My only regret was that I didn't compete in the British Open at the Old Course in St. Andrews. I was on a roll, and St. Andrews, with its premium on shotmaking, suited my game perfectly.

But at that time, the U.S. Open champ did not receive an invite to the British Open. The entry deadline was in May, but I was broke. (The Royal and Ancient Golf Club of St. Andrews changed the rules later, granting the U.S. Open winner an automatic exemption. Tony Lema won the Open that I missed. Ironically, I gave Lema some advice just before he made the trip. "If you're in position to win," I told Lema, "remember this one thing. Don't you ever hit a wedge at 18. You run it up the valley. Trust me. That's the way to win in style.")

I didn't believe that my hard work on the range was the sole reason for my inspired play. I felt then, as I do now, that God played a vital role. He answered my prayers and gave me another chance, and I would be forever grateful. I was playing so well, in fact, that I started to get back some of that old cockiness. I became totally convinced that Lema and I had enough game to challenge the highly touted "Big Three" of Palmer, Nicklaus, and Player. I discussed the idea with my promoter, the incomparable Fred Corcoran.

"Five exhibitions, $50,000, winner take all," I told Corcoran. "We can beat them."

Corcoran approached Mark McCormack, the agent who represented the Big Three. He told McCormack he could set up five matches, including one at Winged Foot.

"You think I'm crazy?" McCormack said. "I've been building the Big Three. If those two guys beat my guys, I have no case."

In late October, I took on one of the Big Three in the Piccadilly World Match Play Championship at the Wentworth

Club in England. My opponent in the third round was Gary Player. Making the field was one of the fringe benefits of my outstanding season. I was looking forward to the challenge. I was also still upset about the incident two years earlier in Canada.

Player and I were having a good match when I suddenly started to lose the feel for my clubs. Must be the weather, I presumed, which of course featured the typical British Isles elements—cold, wind, and rain.

But after hitting a thin 3 iron, I looked down at my hands. What I saw then I would see again and again over the ensuing years. The ends of my fingers were white and forming blisters, only with no water. I could peel the skin right off. "What the hell is going on?" I wondered.

I finished the match, which I lost 4 and 2. The match, of course, was the last thing on my mind. But as the days wore on, I did nothing about it. I was the type who only went to the doctor as a last resort. It will go away, I kept telling myself. It will go away.

Only it didn't go away. Whenever my hands got cold, the peeling would start all over again. During a television match a month later with Mike Souchak in Palm Springs, I put my hands on a generator and, believe it or not, couldn't feel a thing. That was the final straw. I couldn't postpone going to the doctor any longer. After making a few calls, I went to see a prominent specialist in Los Angeles. He suggested that I might have contracted Raynaud's Phenomenon, a circulatory disorder, and put me on cortisone. My hands didn't improve, but at least I was finally doing something about it.

Meanwhile, I kept playing. I needed the money, as usual. But that wasn't the sole motivation. The other had to do with the most fragile of male possessions, the ego. I was one of the top players in the world again for the first time in four long, painful years. I was the old Venturi, with visions of greater stardom. The last thing I was willing to do was skip more tournaments and lose my edge. I had skipped enough tournaments already.

In the fall of 1964, I was the most decorated individual in the game, the Player of the Year, and *Sports Illustrated*'s Sportsman of the Year, outpolling such impressive athletes as baseball's Ken Boyer, Olympic swimmer Don Schollander, and Baltimore Colts quarterback Johnny Unitas. The honor meant a lot to me, as did the award itself, a Grecian urn dating back to 510 B.C. I went to one dinner after another, basking in all the attention, hoping it would last forever.

In January 1965 I played in the Los Angeles Open and the Crosby . . . if you can call it playing. In eight rounds I failed to break 70. Going to Pebble Beach was an especially ill-advised idea. The cold weather was the worst thing for my hands. A few days later I went back to the doctor in Los Angeles, who put me through more tests and sent me to the hospital for a biopsy. But they couldn't come up with a definite diagnosis, which worried me. I've always been at my best when I can identify the opponent.

I had never faced an opponent like this. It followed me everywhere. On the course, the clubs fell from my hands without my knowledge. Off the course, I dropped glasses, books, keys, and other objects. Only the sound of them hitting the ground told me what happened. I stopped carrying anything too valuable. I looked awful, as well. The cortisone made my face bloated and swollen, as if I weighed over 300 pounds. The swelling in my fingers was so bad, I was beginning to wonder whether this "specialist" knew what he was doing. But sports medicine was in such a primitive state. Today, I would seek a second and third opinion before taking any drugs.

I planned to follow the tour to Florida, figuring the warm weather would be the perfect remedy.

But, if anything, my hands became worse. There was no way I could compete at a serious level. I couldn't stop wondering: why was God putting me through another test?

Even so, I wasn't going to miss The Masters, not again. I had worked so hard to earn my way back after the rejection of a year earlier. I wasn't about to let anything, even common sense, get in the way. My resiliency, however, was no match for this mysterious ailment. I played so miserably in a practice round that Mike Souchak, my playing partner, consistently outdrove me, and I was never known as a short hitter. There was no strength in my hands. Forget about the 13th and 15th holes. I had trouble reaching a few of the *par-4s* in two! In the tournament, I shot rounds of 77 and 80, missing the cut by a mile. Players asked me what was wrong. I didn't tell them. I wasn't about to start making excuses now.

After The Masters, I finally decided to seek a second opinion at the Mayo Clinic in Rochester, Minnesota. I finally got some answers. Dr. James Ross said I was suffering from carpal tunnel syndrome, which is when the band around the wrist presses against the tendons, pinching the nerves. The possible cause? Hitting thousands and thousands of practice balls over 20 years.

My timing was terrible. Today, carpal tunnel is often treated on an outpatient basis. Doctors stabilize the affected area with a splint and offer excellent chances for a complete recovery. In 1965, the chances of a complete recovery were not excellent. In my case, it would require surgery on both wrists, and soon. My hands were only going to get worse.

There was another problem. For the prior three months, I had taken too many doses of cortisone, 16 milligrams per day, to be exact. The doctors at the Mayo Clinic were shocked. The highest daily intake they could discover in their records was eight milligrams. The dosage I was taking could have done serious damage. Today, there would be dozens of lawyers at my door anxious to sue the doctor who treated me. After my last visit to the Mayo Clinic, he asked to see me. I did, although I'm not sure why. He had the nerve, believe it or not, to send me a bill for an office visit. I never paid him, needless to say.

The doctors in Minnesota said I needed to be broken down to about one-half milligram per day before they would be able to operate. Going cold turkey was too risky. I could have the surgery in late May.

So what did I do? I delayed it, of course, for about a month. My stubborn pride interfered with sound reasoning. The U.S. Open at Bellerive Country Club in St. Louis was slated for the middle of June and, more than anything else, I wanted to defend my title. In hindsight, I should have had the operation sooner. There was no chance for me to win the Open, and every chance for me to lose the feeling in my hands for good. For almost 40 years, I've lived with a mystery I will never solve: would a few weeks have made a difference?

Going through cortisone withdrawal was a horrible experience. There was one violent episode after another. I was told the violence was always directed against myself, thank goodness. I often became hysterical. I don't remember and I'm glad.

The most frightening moment took place in Akron, shortly before the Open. I was in town to play an exhibition with Souchak at Portage Country Club. On the way to the course, noticing we were about to run into a wall, I quickly put on the brakes and the car spun around. I had saved us from a potentially fatal accident, but there was one problem—there was no wall. I had invented one in my mind, another result of the cortisone withdrawal. Incredibly, nobody was hurt. Souchak took the wheel and brought me to the club. I still went to St. Louis. The only concession I made was to put benzoin, a type of resin, on my palm and fingers to keep the clubs from falling out of my hands. Now if I could only keep a firm grip on my sanity.

In St. Louis I did hit a wall, shooting rounds of 81 and 79, not even close to making the cut. The way I saw it, though, I made the grade by showing up. I was in tremendous pain, but there was no way I would quit. The way I was going, it seemed pretty certain that I would never defend an Open title again. (The 1965 Open, incidentally, was the first to be held without the traditional 36-hole Saturday finish. My ordeal at Congressional in 1964 was cited officially as the reason for the change, which I've always disputed. The real reason was television and the potential for higher ratings and more revenue. I was fortunate to play 36 holes in one day. If I had slept on my third-round 66, I might have gone out the following day without the same determined state of mind. Hogan, in my opinion, also benefited from 36-hole finishes. With his dogged attitude, he beat other players down mentally, a more difficult task in just 18 holes. I contend he might not have won four Open titles.)

On Saturday morning, Charley Johnson and Sonny Randle, friends who played for the St. Louis Cardinals football team, drove me to the airport. I flew straight to Minnesota. I could delay the operation no longer. Was I terrified? You bet. But I also knew that surgery represented my best hope of being a competitive player again. On Monday, I was put on the table and into the capable hands of Dr. Edward Henderson. With any luck, my hands soon would be capable, as well.

The operation went pretty well, they told me, although it would be weeks, maybe months, before anyone could be certain. The left hand recovered a lot faster than the right. They cut a little too deeply into the right wrist, causing a scar to grow around the median nerve. For the first time in my career, I demonstrated a quality I didn't know I possessed—patience. There was no sense in playing again until I was ready.

While I waited, I received many letters of encouragement. One is particularly memorable:

> . . . When finally you win your bout with the doctors, I am sure that you will again have many opportunities to claim your skill and sportsmanship. I hope they will come soon . . . sincerely, Dwight Eisenhower.

In September, ready or not, I went back to the course. The Ryder Cup was coming up, another event I was not going to miss. The matches, scheduled for Royal Birkdale in England, were not as big a deal as they have become today, but they were a big deal for me, and, for that matter, the rest of the squad. I become very upset when some of the current players act as if they, or perhaps their most immediate predecessors, invented the Ryder Cup. I have a news bulletin for them: they didn't.

From the moment I turned pro in November of 1956, being selected for the team was one of my primary goals. In the fifties, a player was required to wait five years before he was eligible to gain points, one of the archaic rules, such as waiting six months to collect official prize money, that I was never able to comprehend. As a result, I lost out on chances to make the squad in 1957, 1959, and 1961. I didn't want to lose out on another chance. With my hand troubles, I knew it could very well be my last chance.

At first, because of my injuries, I was asked to be the captain in 1965. No thanks, I said. I wanted to play. I thought I would be the captain some other year. The assignment instead went to Byron Nelson.

Fortunately, my hands started to improve just in time. I was pleasantly surprised at how well I was striking the ball only three months after the surgery. I felt sure I would do a good job representing my country.

But in England the weather turned cold, and so did my game. I lost my singles match to Peter Alliss, 3 and 1, which, thankfully, didn't have any effect on the outcome. With such stars as Palmer, Lema, Boros, Casper, and Littler—Jack Nicklaus hadn't been on the tour long enough to qualify yet—the United States easily out-dueled Great Britain and Ireland, $19^1/_2$ to $12^1/_2$. The Ryder Cup was very one-sided in those days.

For me, the highlight of the week came in the match between Lema and myself against Bernard Hunt and Neil Coles. We were 1 up coming to the last hole, but soon found trouble.

I faced an almost impossible pitch shot. There was a bunker between me and the pin and almost no green to work with. Going to the back of the green would leave a very difficult two-putt. If that wasn't challenging enough, our opponents were sitting pretty, in range to secure an easy two-putt.

One observer, prejudiced in favor of the other side, was feeling pretty confident. Nelson later told me about their conversation. "Well, Mr. Nelson, I think you're in a bit of trouble," said Harold

Wilson, the British prime minister. "Our men are on the green. This match could be halved."

Nelson turned to him.

"Mr. Prime Minister, I don't mean any disrespect," he said, "but I've got a lot of men on this team, and if I had to pick one man to hit this shot, he's hitting it right now." I executed the sand wedge perfectly and the ball finished close to the hole. We were able to halve the hole, and won the match 1 up.

"Well, well, Mr. Nelson," the prime minister added, "you do know your men."

A few weeks later, I tied for 35th at the Almaden Open Invitational in San Jose. There was nothing particularly memorable about that tournament, except perhaps in one regard: I cashed a check, my first of the year. The money wasn't fabulous, $295, but it sure beat going home with nothing.

It marked the end of the 1965 season. I thought that 1961, 1962, and 1963 had been difficult years, but they were banner years compared to 1965. What made my decline even tougher to accept was how it could happen on the heels of the wonderful comeback in 1964. I felt that, in a manner of months, I went from the *Sports Illustrated* Sportsman of the Year to the FBI Witness Protection Program.

What could be next?

When things weren't going so well on the golf course, I had a tendency to retreat to the racetrack. I suppose I could have found a safer pastime, but I loved racing those cars. Photo courtesy of G. N. Pendleton.

Talking golf with Bing Crosby at Pebble Beach in the mid-sixties.

The 1965 Ryder Cup team. My bad hands combined with the damp, cold weather at Royal Birkdale didn't make for exceptional play on my part, but fortunately our team was strong enough that we managed to win the Cup easily that year. Left to right, in the front row, are Tony Lema, Gene Littler, captain Byron Nelson, Tommy Jacobs, and Arnold Palmer. In the back, from left to right, are Dave Marr, Julius Boros, Don January, Johnny Pott, Billy Casper, and myself. Photo courtesy of Bill Mark.

Oh, to be back home again! This was my reaction after sinking the final putt to win the 1966 Lucky International at good old Harding Park Course in San Francisco. With my friends and family in the gallery, it was one of my most satisfying victories—and the last of my career. Photo courtesy of AP/Wide World Photos.

Ready to take a ride in the 427 Shelby Cobra with son Tim. I purchased the car from its designer, Carroll Shelby.

Relaxing on the patio in Palm Springs with my other son, Matt, during his teenage years. Photo courtesy of Bill Mark.

Beau and me at a castle in Ireland in the mid-nineties.

For several years, Frank Sinatra and I were truly inseparable. It was only after Beau and I moved from Palm Springs to Florida that we slowly, and sadly, fell out of touch with him.

When Ben Hogan, the master himself, took time out to give advice to Harvie Ward and myself, we made sure not to miss a word.

A visit with President George Bush and his family at their place on Walker's Point in Kennebunkport, Maine. That's former White House photographer Susan Biddle between me and my longtime broadcast partner and dear friend, Jim Nantz.

Our 2000 Presidents Cup team tries on some patriotic gear for motivation. Not only did we win the Cup, but we won it in record fashion.

Captaining our country's Presidents Cup team to victory in 2000 was one of the most enjoyable and rewarding experiences I have ever had in the game of golf.

Kathleen and me on our wedding day on March 24, 2003. Jim and Lou Langley were our witnesses.

I have been wonderfully blessed not only to have played and lived the game I love all my life, but also to have found true love not once, but twice.

Chapter Fourteen

TWO FRANKS AND
ONE BEAU

I remained hopeful despite everything. I had emerged from hibernation before. There was no reason to believe I couldn't do it again. I would have to work harder than I did in 1963, but so what? I loved going to the range, as it brought back memories of my youth at Harding Park when it was just me and my dreams. Many had come true. Many had not.

In late January of 1966, I was back at Harding, competing in the tour's Lucky International Open. I still had my dreams. After a respectable showing at the Los Angeles Open—I tied for 28th— I was hoping that a return to familiar soil would spark a return to familiar form. I wanted so much to play well in front of my family and friends, who had supported me through my terrible ordeal.

The week started in great fashion. During the pro-am at the 8th hole, a 189-yard par-3, I hit a 3 iron that took a few bounces . . . right into the hole! The gallery went nuts, especially one lady who ran on the green and took the ball out of the hole. One of the amateurs in my group, the low-handicapper, said something he would soon regret.

"Who the hell is that dumb s.o.b. running out on the green and waving the ball around?" he said.

I took a long pause. I should have been an actor.

"If I'm not mistaken," I told him, "I think that's my mother."

The poor amateur was not the same again. He apologized and nearly whiffed the next shot. Yet with my ace and an eagle on the last hole, our team edged out another for first place. They had already given the prizes away and had to take them back.

The ace was a good omen. I shot a 68 in the first round, hitting, I believe, every green in regulation. The weather was balmy, especially for the Bay Area, which kept my hands from becoming too stiff. I could feel the club, which made all the difference. I followed with another 68 in the second round, overcoming slightly cooler conditions. I was overjoyed. I hadn't fired two consecutive rounds in the 60s since the tournament in Portland 16 long months earlier. I was in contention. I had forgotten what that feeling was like.

But on Saturday I started to lose the feeling in my hands. The weather got colder and started to pour, the worst possible combination for me. With each hole, my hopes slipped further away. On the 6th, while contemplating this cruel change by Mother Nature, we received word that play was canceled for the day. Bottom line: those five holes never happened and I was back in the tournament. I didn't waste my mulligan, shooting an even-par 71 on the following day to tie Palmer, four strokes behind Frank Beard.

For the final round, I was paired with Terry Dill. Although I started strong, making the turn in 33, I was unable to gain a shot on Beard, who was in the group behind us. I was quickly running out of holes—and tolerance. The only way I survived was with the assistance of my father and uncle, who placed buckets of hot water on the backs of several carts. Every other hole, while waiting on the tee, I put my hands in the water and wiped them off. I also put on gloves and used a hand warmer while walking down the fairways.

After pars on 10, 11, 12, and 13, I converted a long birdie putt at 14. At 16, a 320-yard dogleg par-4, I received a tremendous break. My plan was to be conservative and lay up with a 2 iron, which would leave me with only a wedge to the green. But when I arrived at the tee, my caddie and longtime friend Bud Allio was already 150 yards down the fairway, leaving me with only one club, the driver.

I was tempted to shout, but I decided against it, not wanting to embarrass Bud, who was also from San Francisco. So I hit the driver—boy did I hit it! The ball traveled about 270 yards and ended up in perfect position just short of the green. I chipped on, and made a putt for the birdie that put me in the lead over Beard. That was the margin I needed, prevailing by a shot over Beard and two over Palmer and three other players. When I came off the green, I was greeted by the type of ovation I wondered if I would ever hear again. I found my father and prepared to give him a hug. Before I could, he put his hands up.

"Your mother is over there," he said, pointing to the proud woman in tears. I hugged her first and then returned to hug my father. I hugged everyone, it seemed.

A few minutes later, I saw Palmer.

"You were a mean son of a gun out there today," said Palmer, who had observed me from adjacent fairways. "I've never seen anyone so focused."

"This is my hometown, Arnold," I said. "It doesn't look like I have a lot of time left to continue my game. This may be my last hurrah. I wanted to win, but I really wanted you more than anything I wanted in the world."

"It showed," he said.

"I'm glad you noticed," I said.

I wasn't kidding about my last hurrah. While my hands improved again, good enough for me to play, I didn't possess the same feel, the same rhythm. I shot only one competitive round in the 60s from February through May. But in June the tour returned to San Francisco, to the Olympic Club, for the U.S. Open. To say I was pumped up would be the understatement of all time. In 1955, the last time our national championship was played at Olympic, I was in Austria. I wasn't going to miss this one.

I spent much of the week with Hogan, creating memories I will always cherish. With my injuries and his increasingly rare appearances on the tour, Hogan and I hadn't played together in ages. On Tuesday and Wednesday, we practiced at California Golf Club. He preferred to be away from the fans and the press. At the Olympic Club, we were paired together for the first two rounds.

When he saw me on the first tee, he looked down at my hands. They were as white as a sheet and cold.

"What the hell is the matter with you?" he said.

"My hands are not doing very good, Ben," I said. "Don't worry about it. I'll get by."

We didn't refer to the issue again, but I could see the look of genuine concern in his eyes and hear it in the sound of his voice. He was the toughest, meanest competitor I've ever encountered, but there was a tremendous amount of warmth in that man. The experts complain about how Hogan was such a heartless individual. To those "experts," I have only one thing to say: you didn't know him. Another time, when I told him about the difficulties I was having with my right hand, he said, "You're very lucky that it's your right hand and not your left, because everyone knows this is a left-handed game." The exact reverse was true. He winked and smiled at me.

Hogan was vulnerable, more than people would ever imagine. During the 1966 Open, he was standing over a 15-footer on the second hole of the first round. Suddenly, he started to shake. I couldn't believe it—Ben Hogan shaking over a putt! It got worse. He froze. I had heard he was having problems on the greens but I didn't know they would be this bad. He stopped and walked over to where I was standing. His eyes were dead.

"I can't draw it back," he told me.

I didn't know what to do. This was Ben Hogan. What do you tell Ben Hogan when he says he can't draw the putter back?

Only one thing, I realized. The truth.

"Who gives a shit?" I said, standing right in his face. "You've beaten people long enough."

His eyes suddenly came to life, and he was able to hit the putt. He almost made it, in fact. Going down the fifth fairway, he thanked me.

"For what?" I said.

"You know what for," he said.

When we finished the round, Hogan asked me to come with him to the locker room. "I don't want anybody to be with us right now," he told the attendant. "Nobody."

"You're the only person in the world who could have said that to me," he said. "I'll never forget that as long as I live."

I downplayed the whole incident because I didn't want Hogan to feel bad. "I probably said the same thing to you that you would have said to me," I told him.

I didn't do too poorly in the tournament, tying for 17th, although well behind Billy Casper and Arnold Palmer. Palmer, in a collapse that has been well chronicled, was headed to certain victory until he squandered a seven-shot lead with nine holes to play, losing the next day to Casper in an 18-hole playoff. Palmer never faltered like that when I was chasing him. Hogan, for the record, finished 12th.

From San Francisco I went to the Western Open in Chicago. I finished ninth, my best showing since January. My game was coming around just in time for my last major of the season, the PGA at Firestone Country Club. The course was one of my favorites, and the site of my most impressive victory ever, the 1964 American Golf Classic. I played well again, but not well enough, coming in 15th, 10 strokes behind winner Al Geiberger. I was feeling a little down until the real world provided me with true sorrow.

I remember the day vividly. Late Sunday afternoon, I confronted my longtime friend, Tony Lema, in the locker room. Lema, I had been told, planned to skip a dinner that was arranged in his honor by a local Italian-American club. I was very disappointed in him.

"What are you doing?" I said. "You promised these people you would be there."

"I'm going to an outing in Illinois," he said. "They're giving me $2,000. They're flying Betty [his wife] and me up there. I'm going where the money is."

I went from disappointment to disgust.

"I don't care how much money you're getting," I argued. "You gave your word to these people. You can't back out now."

My plea did no good.

"You will live to regret those words," I said.

I left for dinner. A few hours later, I returned to my hotel. When I walked in to pick up my keys, the clerk at the counter gave me the news.

"It's too bad about that golfer who got killed today," she said.

She didn't tell me the name and I didn't ask. Somehow I knew. On the night of Al Geiberger's victory in the 1966 PGA, Lema, 32, was killed in a plane crash along with his wife, the pilot, and the copilot.

In 1967, there was another accident. One day my seven-year-old son, Tim, was riding his bicycle down a driveway on our street. I had told him over and over not to ride his bike in that area. "We'll put it in the car," I said, "and you can ride around in the park." He didn't listen. Coming down the hill, he was hit by a truck with a hook mounted on it—the hook struck him in the mouth. He required 220 stitches and underwent several plastic surgeries to save his face. He was very fortunate to be alive. A split second sooner and the truck would have run him over.

Tim stayed in the hospital for weeks. I stuck around when he came home. This was no time to be thinking of myself. Needless to say, the tension in the house was unbearable. Some couples find a way to rally around tragedy and become closer. We were not one of those couples.

In late spring, I finally rejoined the tour. I was no better off than I had been during most of 1966. My right hand showed a lot of atrophy. The hand would never be the same again. I tried to play, but 1967 became another lost year. There were far too many of them already.

Soon it was 1968, one of the most turbulent years in our nation's history. Everything seemed to be falling apart: our institutions, our values, our families, our hopes of a better tomorrow.

I tried not to get too caught up in it, as I was consumed enough with my own failures. From January through June, I recorded only one top 50 finish, a tie for 46th at The Masters. My career was in more jeopardy than ever.

In early July, I arrived in Grand Blanc, Michigan, for the Buick Open Invitational, a few miles from where I made my first official start in 1957, when I saw so much in front of me. Now I saw nothing in front of me. Early in the week, Frank Chirkinian, the producer of golf coverage for CBS, said he wanted to talk to me. What for, I couldn't begin to imagine. Certainly not to ask me to be one of the participants in the CBS Golf Classic. Not if the network was interested in good ratings.

"Ken, how would you like to do some television?" Chirkinian asked.

Me do television? Didn't he know I was the guy who stammered? With a lot of hard work, the problem was under control to some extent. But put me on live television and anything could happen.

Of course, Chirkinian knew, yet he wasn't dissuaded. He told me I had something to offer, though, to this day, I believe the real reason was that he felt sorry for me. He probably thought I was done. A lot of people thought I was done.

I turned him down at first. Even if he wasn't concerned that I would make a fool of myself, I was. But he was persistent, a trait I would see him display over and over for almost 30 years. Fine, I told him, I'll give it a try. Only what do I say?

"If I have to tell you what to say," Chirkinian responded, "then you'll have to get out of the business. You say anything you want to say, but there is something you should remember. You're doing TV. It's not what you say, it's what you don't say. Never say the obvious."

In my audition I was asked to analyze the swing of Rocky Thompson, a journeyman on the tour. I complimented his address position, and then Chirkinian proceeded to show Thompson's swing in slow motion. But when I talked about his takeaway, downswing, and finish, I purposely said everything backward. I didn't know any other way to explain it.

"Look how straight he keeps his left arm," I said. His arm was bent.

"Look how he keeps his left heel on the ground." He picked his left heel up about three inches.

"Look how he starts his downswing right on line and keeps the flex in his knees." He was spinning out.

I thought Chirkinian and everyone in the truck was going to die of laughter. Thompson, to put it gently, did not possess a picturesque swing.

"You're totally nuts," Chirkinian said. "You got the job."

I was on the air sporadically in that first year, still not fully prepared—isn't the player always the last to know?—to give up tournament golf. But with one mediocre performance after another—I didn't break 70 the whole year, for goodness sake—even I was beginning to wake up.

In those days, I spent a lot of time in Palm Springs with a new friend, Frank Sinatra. Many people never became aware of our relationship, which was just the way I liked it. I didn't want to become another fringe character who loses favor after revealing too much about the inner circle. I was tested, in fact, on more than one occasion. Sinatra's people would plant snippets of inaccurate information that could be traced to only one source. I passed every time.

Once in Las Vegas, Sinatra, myself, and a few others were playing a game of blackjack. I sat next to Sinatra.

"Why don't you bet for me, too?" asked Sinatra, who pushed $5,000 in chips in my direction and continued to play. With my own money, I had been betting about $50 a hand.

I cashed in my chips and started to bet with his chips at $500 a hand. Looking down at that kind of money, I couldn't help but think how much it would come in handy.

"I've had enough of this," Sinatra said a half hour later. "Let's cash in and go have a drink."

I pushed the chips toward him. I had won about $20,000.

"No, that's yours," he said. "You won it."

"Francis, it wasn't my money," I told him. I pushed the chips toward the dealer. "These are Mr. Sinatra's," I said, and left the table.

While we were walking to the bar, Sinatra grabbed my arm and kissed me on the cheek.

"There aren't many people like you," he said.

He always called me Kenneth, and I always called him Francis. We went everywhere together. One night, about an hour after he drove me home, the phone rang.

"What are you doing?" Sinatra said.

"I'm going to bed," I said. "You just dropped me off."

"Let's go to New York," he suggested. "I'll pick you up in 45 minutes."

Was I going to say no? To Frank Sinatra? You have got to be kidding. In 45 minutes, I was picked up in his Rolls. We flew to the Big Apple in his private plane—me, Francis, and his body-guard, Jilly Rizzo. For three days we lived it up in typical Sinatra style: the best restaurants, the best clubs, the best of everything. Another time, we took a train from San Bernardino, California, to

Chicago, where he was going to give a New Year's Eve concert. When we arrived in Chicago, the time came to thank the help. Sinatra handed me his money clip. "Take care of them," he said. "They were great."

"What do you want to pay them?" Jilly asked me.

"Who cares?" I said. "It's not our money." I laughed and gave him a wink.

I gave three of them $300 apiece, and one of them, the big man, $500. When Sinatra showed up a few minutes later, I gave him his money clip. The workers all said the same thing: "Mr. Sinatra, thank you very much." Each time, he responded: "It's quite all right." When Sinatra started to leave, the head man grabbed him by the arm.

"I knows now why dae call *you* da King," he said.

The look on Sinatra's face was priceless. "What the hell did you tip those guys?" he asked.

"Who cares?" I said. "They called you the King, didn't they?"

He was certainly the King in my mind, no matter what was written over the years about his ties to the gambling world. Frankly, I had never judged a person by someone else's opinion, and I wasn't about to change that practice with Sinatra.

In my opinion, similar to Hogan, another misunderstood man, Sinatra was incredibly compassionate. When we lived together for three months—the house I had purchased was being redone—he would sift through the newspaper every morning to look for people he could help. There would be only one condition: nobody could say the help came from him. When Toots Shor was down and out, Sinatra, Jilly, and I went to visit him when we were in New York. When we left the restaurant, Sinatra handed him $50,000 in cash.

Sinatra and I played a lot of golf, although I don't recall him ever going a full 18 holes. The game frustrated him, and so, at times, did playing with me.

"You know what I get tired of you doing?" he said. "Telling me, 'Francis, nice drive. Francis, good shot.' We get up to our balls and you're 100 yards ahead of me."

"OK," I said, "do you want me to sing a few bars for you?"

"No, no," he said, "you keep playing golf and I'll sing."

When we were out on the town, I made it a point to never sit next to Sinatra. There were other people, including some pretty big Hollywood names, who would jockey for that position. I sat at the other end of the table. But when my side of the table was having a good time, Sinatra would get curious. He didn't want to miss anything, especially when comedian Pat Henry was around. Henry often opened for Sinatra.

"What's so funny?" Sinatra would say. "Nobody is laughing over at my end."

One activity we did not do together was chase women, yet Sinatra played a very prominent role in the story of the one woman I did chase, the first woman I ever really loved.

In 1967, I was in Palm Springs to prepare for the upcoming season. One evening I drove downtown to meet Sinatra for dinner at Ruby's Dunes, the in-place. Pick any night of the week and you were guaranteed to spot a Hollywood star. When I walked in on this particular night, I spotted a star, all right—at least in my eyes, if not of the silver screen. Wearing an orange dress, standing no more than five feet tall, she was the most beautiful thing I had ever seen. Her name was Beau.

Beau, who worked as the hostess, walked right up to me. She was a woman who wasn't afraid of anything, even of death, as I would later discover. We talked for quite a while, and the chemistry between us was a powerful force I didn't know could exist. I fell in love that very instant and so did she. Unfortunately, there was nothing either of us could do about it. Both of us were married. They were difficult marriages, to be certain, but we were married, nonetheless. Fooling around was not an option. We said good night to each other and that was that.

I thought about Beau a lot, especially as it was becoming more apparent with each passing day that Conni and I would never patch things up. I thought about her warmth, her humor, the strong feeling that we should be together. I considered calling her, but I knew the timing wasn't right. I began to wonder if the timing would ever be right. In early 1968, a full year after we met, I couldn't worry about the timing any longer. I went back to Ruby's, not knowing if she would be there. My heart was beating louder than ever. Before then, I thought pressure was lining up a downhill eight-footer at Augusta National. Now I found out what pressure really felt like.

I walked inside and there she was, in the exact same spot, taking reservations, even more striking than I remembered. We gave each other hugs and felt the chemistry all over again. Beau and I talked for a long time that evening, telling our life stories and starting new ones, both aware that nothing would ever be the same again.

Chapter Fifteen

MORE CHANGES

In 1970, I went to Akron, Ohio, to see Dr. Walter Hoyt, one of the nation's most distinguished orthopedic surgeons. I was still searching for one more miracle, one more chance to see what I could do with two good hands. I had met Dr. Hoyt a few years earlier at Portage Country Club, when my right hand began to develop atrophy again. He had recommended a combination of therapy and rest in hope that the tendons would properly heal. But this time he told me therapy and rest would not be enough. I would need an operation, and that wasn't the worst of it. If the operation didn't go well, there was a good chance I could lose parts of three fingers on my right hand.

"Go home and get all your business in order, Ken," he told me.

I got my business in order, if not my emotions. I was scared more than ever before. Why was this happening? I wondered. Why now, why me, after all I had proven?

I saw my dad in San Francisco before the operation. Although we were close, he was never the kind to shower me with praise. That was my mother's job, which, I might add, she did quite well.

I wasn't mad at him. If anything, I was grateful. He kept me constantly motivated, determined to prove myself. I never wanted to let him down.

The visit was wonderful. Soon, too soon, I told him I had to go. While he drove me to the airport, I shared my deepest fears about the operation, about the very real possibility that I would never play golf again. He listened for the longest time, and then he spoke.

"Son, it doesn't matter if you ever play again," he said.

"How can you say that, Dad?" I responded. After all, those words were coming from the man who had told me to never quit, that it was the only thing in life that didn't require any talent.

"Because, Son," he said, "you were the best I ever saw."

My fears were gone. My dad told me I was the best he ever saw. I could face anything.

The operation took almost four hours, as Dr. Hoyt and his assistants essentially built me a new right hand. When the operation ended he told me some good news and some bad news. The good news was that my fingers would be spared. The bad news was that my career wouldn't be so fortunate. When asked if I would ever play golf again, Dr. Hoyt replied, "Ken, you'll always be able to play golf, but not up to your standards."

The news should have crushed me. In another time, another place, it *would* have crushed me. But, with Beau's love and my father's praise, I was able to cope. I also thought back to the morning in my basement six years earlier when all seemed lost forever, when I prayed to God: "Do with me what you will, but please give me one more chance. I promise I will find a way to give back." God gave me one more chance, a chance that changed my life, and now, apparently, it was time for me to fulfill my part of the bargain.

First things first. I needed a new source of revenue, and in a hurry. My finances were so precarious that I was forced to sell one of my most prized possessions, an original 427 Shelby Cobra I had purchased from its inventor, Caroll Shelby. I felt like I was caught in some bizarre shell game, constantly moving my debts from one place to another to stay one step ahead of the collectors. Thank goodness for Frank Chirkinian, who said I could sign a full-time contract with CBS if I left the tour.

Before I could say yes, I had to check with Dr. Cary Middlecoff, the man I would be replacing. I respected Middlecoff. I also thought back to how Dave Marr took over the Jantzen endorsement in 1964 without bothering to run it by me first. I sure wasn't going to do that to Middlecoff. I joined him for a martini in his hotel room during the tournament in Ohio.

"Doc, I've got to ask you something," I said. "CBS has offered me your job."

"I knew they would," he said. "We're having a few problems. You go ahead and take it. I don't want it."

"I had to ask you," I said. "I wouldn't go behind your back."

Weeks later, he called me.

"I'm so taken back," he said. "They told me you wouldn't take it unless I gave my blessing."

There was one possession I would not sell—my U.S. Open medal. One day, I received an anonymous call from a man offering me $350,000. He told me another Open champion recently sold his medal to someone else, and now he wanted mine. "Don't call back," I assured him. "There is no number you can give me. I will not sell." I have never, for a second, regretted that decision. Of course, the 350 grand could have fixed all my problems, but it would have also created new ones I could never fix. My reputation was not for sale to the highest bidder, not after all the work I put in to rebuild it.

My marriage, however, was beyond rebuilding. Conni and I had been separated for many months, although neither of us made any move toward arranging a formal divorce. I don't know what we were waiting for. Conni was moving on in her life, as I was in mine. She even hosted a party at our house on the very day I was having my operation in Akron. When I returned to San Francisco, she let it all out.

"I want to tell you something," she said. "I've got other things I want to do. You're broke, you're busted, and you can't play golf anymore. I want a divorce."

She was feeling pretty proud of herself . . . for about two seconds, until I delivered my response.

"You got it," I said. "I'm glad you said that because I have already filed for divorce."

"You s.o.b.," she said.

"I guess I did the right thing," I said.

In truth, I had not filed for divorce. The only reason I lied was that I wasn't going to allow her to think she had defeated me. This, I suppose, was match play of the cruelest kind, and, like always, I was determined to win.

Either way, we were finally putting an end to a much greater lie—our marriage. As for our kids, Matt, 14, chose to live with me while Tim, 11, stayed with Conni by court order. But as the months dragged on, Tim decided he wanted to live with his father and brother, and so he did. I was grateful to have all of us under the same roof again.

I paid Conni a fairly substantial alimony every month, though, in her opinion, not substantial enough. She took me back to court and asked the judge to raise the alimony, which he did. When I started to make more money, Conni figured she ought to receive her share. So she took me to court again. This time, however, I was going to take a stand. Even so, there were limits to how I would fight. When my lawyer announced in court that he wanted to put Matt and Tim on the stand to testify, the judge looked down at me.

"You want to bring his sons into court?" the judge asked, taking a quick glance at my lawyer.

Then, with the judge looking in my direction for a moment—my lawyer couldn't see me—I slowly shook my head, no. No matter how I felt about Conni, she was still the mother of our children. To me, putting Matt and Tim in that position didn't seem right.

The judge gave me a nod.

"There will be no need to have the children come to court," he said. "You understand this is the third time that both of you have come to court? You must accept my decision." Lawyers for both sides agreed.

A few days later, the judge was ready to deliver his decision.

"Now let me get this straight," the judge said. "The father has the children?"

Yes, each lawyer agreed.

"And the father pays child support?" Yes again, the lawyers said, mentioning how I was still paying even though the children were living with me.

"What about medical care, schooling, and insurance?" he asked.

The lawyers agreed one more time: I was the one paying the bills.

"Mrs. Venturi, may I ask you something?" the judge said. "What do you do for a living now?"

"I'm unemployed," she said.

"Mrs. Venturi," he said, "Because the father is bearing all the expenses, I suggest you get yourself a job." He announced his decision: "Alimony terminated."

I couldn't believe what I had just heard. I was greatly relieved. At the same time, I knew Conni was upset about the decision, and I felt bad for her. I felt bad about a lot of things that had happened between us over the years.

Beau got along wonderfully with Matt and Tim. My parents also signed up for Beau's fan club.

"Son," my mom said to me, "if you don't marry Beau, I'm going to be so embarrassed that I've raised the dumbest son who ever lived."

Mom wasn't the only one to make sure I received the message.

"If you don't marry her, I think I will," Sinatra said.

I suppose I was ambivalent about marriage after my first experience. I didn't want to ruin what Beau and I were building.

I asked Sinatra to be my best man. He turned me down for a very good reason.

"You can't afford the wedding," he said. "I'll give the bride away [Beau's father had passed away] and give the party."

The wedding, held in Palm Springs on November 13, 1972, was magical, a three-day gathering of family and several hundred friends that I wished could have lasted forever. With Sinatra taking care of every detail, Beau and I were able to concentrate on each other and on the new chapter we couldn't wait to begin. We felt like teenagers going steady.

One chapter starting, another closing. In January of 1973, I went up to the Monterey Peninsula to play in the Crosby. Although "retired," I still competed in a few events each year. With my mother very ill—she was in the latter stages of lung cancer— I hadn't planned to go this time, but she wouldn't hear of it. "That's where you belong," said Mom, who was being treated at the Eisenhower Hospital in Rancho Mirage. "I'll be here when you get back." After we said good-bye to her, Beau and I sat by the fountain in front of the hospital. I began to cry. "I don't think I'll ever see her alive again," I said.

The Crosby, to be sure, meant a lot to me, ever since Bing tracked me down at San Jose State way back in 1952. I would do anything to be in his tournament. I loved being around the likes of Phil Harris, Jack Lemmon, Dean Martin, and all the other celebrities who made it such a tremendous week. In my day the celebrities knew their place. They knew that on the golf course they were on our stage. It is totally different today. (A few years ago, I was in the 18th tower watching Ray Romano make a mess of the 10th hole at Pebble Beach. He was picking up penalty strokes all over the place, touching rocks next to the water, grounding his club, hitting the sand with his club, you name it. Jim Nantz proceeded to do a promo for Romano's show. "Coming up on CBS Monday night, *Everybody Loves Raymond* . . . right Ken?" Nantz said. I didn't miss a beat. "Well, not everybody," I said. I thought Nantz was going to fall out of his chair. Romano came to me later, a little upset. "Hey, if you can be funny on your show," I told him, "I can be funny on mine.")

I was about to hit my first tee shot in 1973 when I saw Beau walking under the ropes. She put her arms around me.

"Mom just died," she said. "What do you want to do?"

I thought of leaving the course, but I realized that playing a round at Pebble Beach would be the most appropriate way to honor her.

"I have to play this round," I told Beau.

My mom had watched me play at Pebble so many times in the past. I put the tee in the ground. "Ma," I said to myself, looking toward the sky, "this round is for you." By my standards, I played very well. Maybe she was watching over me.

I withdrew after the round and made the arrangements for her funeral in San Francisco. The whole city seemed to show up, and I was not surprised. I knew how much she was beloved. Beau and I settled in, taking care of the boys and each other. In July of 1973, I went to Royal Troon to compete in my first and only British Open. I played a few practice rounds with Gene Sarazen, who, at 71, was still a tough competitor. That week, in fact, he aced Troon's "Postage Stamp" eighth hole in the first round. As for me, with unexpectedly balmy weather in the British Isles, I was hitting the ball great. "You've got a chance to win this thing," Sarazen told me. But the next day, the temperature turned so cold that my hands turned white. So much for hitting the ball great.

In 1974, I played in my last U.S. Open, at Winged Foot just outside New York City. I picked quite an Open to make my exit. The United States Golf Association, embarrassed by Johnny Miller's final-round 63 a year before at Oakmont, was determined to make things tougher this time around for the top players in the world. The USGA succeeded. The '74 Open, which became known as "The Massacre at Winged Foot," was won by Hale

Irwin at 7 over par. It was a massacre for me, all right. I shot well over par and did not make the cut.

In the early seventies Beau and I spent a lot of time with Sinatra, who came by almost every week to watch *Monday Night Football*, which, with Howard Cosell, Don Meredith, and Frank Gifford in the booth, was a major social event. Beau made the pasta and Sinatra brought the wine.

There were two nights with Sinatra that will always stand out. The first was his last concert in Las Vegas before he retired. Everybody was there: Tony Bennett, Vic Damone, Dionne Warwick, Sandy Koufax, Don Drysdale, and others. Sinatra introduced the long list of celebrities but didn't mention me. Beau leaned over to me.

"He didn't introduce you," she said.

"Shhh, we know our relationship," I said. "It's not important."

Just then Sinatra paused.

"Before I sing my last song," he said, "I hope I didn't miss anybody, but I have one more person to introduce. You all know him as a great golfer, and you've seen him on television, but I guess the best way to describe him is, 'Ladies and gentlemen, I'd like to introduce you to my brother.'" I stood up. Sinatra leaned over and gave me a kiss. "I'll see you in the back," he said. After the show ended, a stranger stopped me.

"I didn't know you were that close to Sinatra," he said.

"I never met the guy in my life," I said, and walked away.

I was very moved by what Sinatra said. I didn't have a brother. Afterward Beau and I went backstage and then flew with him to Palm Springs, spending the night at his house.

The other story took place some time later. Sinatra was hosting a party with another A-list gathering—Kirk Douglas, Gregory

Peck, Richard Burton, Elizabeth Taylor, just to name a few. After dinner, a handful of us were sitting around a table when I asked Lenny Hayden, the great composer, if he would play a few songs. Sure, Hayden said. He and I walked into the living room and sat at the grand piano. Within moments we were joined by Broadway composer Fritz Lowe and Jimmy van Heusen, the Oscar Award–winning songwriter ("Swinging on a Star," "Call Me Irresponsible," "High Hopes"). A few people gathered around us, recognizing what a treat this was turning into, and the best was yet to come. Sinatra, who never sang in an informal group, went into his bedroom, brought back a whole stack of music, and put it on the piano.

"What's your favorite song?" he said.

Someone named a title. He found the music, sang four or five bars, and asked for another request, and so on. The hours passed quickly, too quickly, as the most accomplished singer in the world gave a free concert in his living room. I felt like I was watching Ben Hogan hit balls in my backyard. I couldn't believe my incredible fortune. At about 4:30 in the morning, Beau and I finally got ready to leave. "That was great," I told Sinatra. "I'm glad you enjoyed it," he said. On our way home I realized what was going on.

"He's going to make a comeback," I told Beau. "Did you see how excited he was to sing again?" A few weeks later, Sinatra made it official.

Meanwhile, around the same time that Sinatra was coming out of retirement, Joe Dey, the commissioner of the PGA Tour, announced he would be going into it. Dey was the one who told me to hold my head up on the final day at Congressional, and, when I couldn't remember my scores, to sign the card.

Dey called me. I could tell that there was more on his mind than small talk. He got to his point.

"Ken, we'd like you to be the commissioner," he said, giving me quite a shock. "The board talked about it, and it was unanimous. We feel that every decision you'd make would be for the betterment of golf and not for individual profit or individual achievement." I was very flattered, to say the least. I thought about how far my reputation had come since the damage caused by the controversy in 1956.

Yet I turned Dey down. Were there problems in the game that I would have loved to address? Absolutely, just as there are problems today that I would love to address. But I was never someone to sit in an office for eight or nine hours a day. That's why my work with Eddie Lowery was so perfect. I could sell a few cars in the morning, have lunch, and be on the tee in the afternoon. Besides, by the mid-seventies, I was busy with my television duties, and I didn't want to deal with the personalities and politics the position would demand. Dey asked me who I would recommend. I mentioned Jay Hebert, but, as we all know, the job went to Deane Beman. Beman turned out to be an excellent choice.

At CBS, in addition to the actual tournament coverage, I did weekly tips, or "stroke savers," as they became more commonly known. The tip we used would often depend on what type of course was hosting the tournament. If, for instance, we were somewhere that placed a high premium on bump-and-run shots near the green, that would be the focus. I usually arrived at the hole about 20 minutes early to hit a few practice shots. With the cameras about to roll, and a gallery of a few hundred assembled, I definitely felt the pressure to perform. I came through, thank goodness, usually needing only one or two takes.

Once, at Hilton Head, I faced a very difficult 40-yard pitch shot over a bunker. On the first take, I got it to within six inches. With the camera still running, Chirkinian said, "You lucky s.o.b., you couldn't hit that again within 20 feet."

"Twenty feet, you say," I said. "Watch this."

I put the ball down, hit in a hurry, and holed out.

"Remember, Frank, if you hit it close, you're good," I said. "If you hit it in the hole, you're lucky."

I owe a lot to Chirkinian, who was quite an innovator, always coming up with the right camera angle, the right amount of lighting, and many of the right tips. Some people in the business were afraid of Chirkinian, calling him the "Ayatollah," but underneath all that bluster he was the sweetest guy in the world. If you did something wrong, and we all did, he would chew you out mercilessly, but the moment the show was over, he forgot about it. The criticism was never personal.

One day, I received a tip from a most unlikely source. I was having lunch at Shady Oaks in Fort Worth with Ben Hogan.

"What's your tip this week?" Hogan asked me.

"I don't know," I said. "Do you have one for me?"

As a matter of fact, he did. Hogan showed me how to put both hands into a weak position when you flip the ball over a bunker, taking the wrists out of the shot. I used his tip that week, saying, without identifying the source, that I received it "from a friend of mine, and it really does work. And, oh, by the way, I still think he's won five Opens." (Hogan is, officially, credited with only four, though in 1942 he won what was called the Hale American Open, cosponsored by the United States Golf Association.)

Another time, at Shady Oaks, Hogan asked: "Do you want to know the secret to golf?" "Of course," I said, "everyone wants to know." "OK," he said, "but you can't tell anyone." "Fine," I promised.

He brought me into the locker room, along with Chirkinian, to demonstrate how, on the backswing, the break in the right arm has to be facing the sky, and on the follow-through, the break in the left arm has to be facing the sky. Both elbows must be pointing to the ground.

"But, remember, you promised not to tell anyone," Hogan said.

"You told me that years ago," I said, "and I have kept your secret, but Chirkinian will tell everyone."

He looked at Chirkinian, and then me.

"Who's going to believe I gave *him* a lesson?" Hogan said.

Hogan possessed a tremendous sense of humor, even if the press failed to notice it. My favorite story is the one involving my former CBS colleague, Gary McCord, which also took place at Shady Oaks, sometime during the late eighties or early nineties. I was about to have lunch with Hogan when Chirkinian and McCord showed up.

After I did the introductions, Hogan asked McCord: "What was your name again?"

"Gary McCord," he said.

"Oh. What do you do?" Hogan continued, after a few words with Chirkinian and me.

"I'm a professional golfer, Mr. Hogan," McCord continued. "I am on the tour and I work for CBS."

Hogan spoke to me for a few more minutes.

"How long have you been on the tour?" he said to McCord.

"Sixteen years, Mr. Hogan," McCord said.

"Oh, what have you won?" Hogan asked.

"Well, actually," McCord said, "I haven't won any tournaments, Mr. Hogan."

"Then, why are you on the tour?" Hogan asked.

McCord could offer no brilliant comeback. "I don't know," he said.

He and Chirkinian soon left.

Hogan turned to me one last time: "What did you say his name was?"

In 1976, Beau and I decided to move to Florida. While Palm Springs provided many wonderful memories, Florida was much closer to most of the tournaments on my television schedule. I would, on occasion, be able to fly out on a Thursday or Friday and be home by Sunday night. A home in Florida would also be more affordable than Palm Springs, one of the most expensive spots in the country. I was making good money, but by no means was I rich.

I was eager, as well, to get far away from what was one of the most distressing experiences of my life. For several years, I had served as director of golf at Mission Hills Country Club in Rancho Mirage, which currently hosts the Nabisco Championship, a major on the LPGA Tour. The job didn't require too many hours and paid decent money. However, because of television, I was away from the course for most of the summer. When I returned one year, I discovered a few of my employees had stolen some of the merchandise. I owed $35,000 to the manufacturers. I paid them all back, though it took me a few years.

Sinatra made one last attempt to convince us to stay. He could be most persuasive.

"I'll pay you," he said. "I'll give you a job." He even offered a spare home we could move into at no charge.

"Frank," I told him, "I can't live like that." (We tried to stay in touch over the phone, but I saw Sinatra on only a few occasions after the mid-seventies. When he became very ill in 1998, Barbara, his wife, called me from Malibu and asked if I would like to visit him. I couldn't bring myself to go. I wanted to remember him as the great man he was.)

Beau and I discovered the perfect lot in Florida on Marco Island, next to the Gulf of Mexico, a place where we could do a lot of fishing and boating. Frank Mackle, a member of the family that practically owned the whole island, offered the land to us for the same price he paid. I was a little hesitant. The property was still a lot of money, and other than television and the work I was doing for Deltona, a land development company, we had no guaranteed income.

"Ken, I know you will make it," he said, sounding like many of the others who had believed in me, even if I hadn't.

Even so, he told me that, in a worst-case scenario, he would buy the home back for the same price. I will always be grateful to Frank Mackle.

I did make it, enjoying more than 25 wonderful years on Marco Island.

Chapter Sixteen

FROM THE TOWER

An even longer relationship was the one I established at CBS. Even today, two years after I bowed out at the Kemper Open, I still can't believe I'm not sitting in the 18th tower anymore.

The talent I worked with over the years was extraordinary, featuring some of the premier names in the business—Jack Whitaker, Vin Scully, Pat Summerall, Ben Wright, Verne Lundquist, Jim Nantz, and the Englishman, Henry Longhurst. I feel sorry for today's younger fans who have never heard Longhurst. Henry, like many during his era, enjoyed a little refreshment. Once, at Augusta, he walked up to the bar in the players' locker room and asked for a martini, straight up. He spilled most of it. He then ordered another, and another, and finally one more. After the fourth martini, not spilling another drop, he thanked the bartender.

"I think it's time to go to work now," he said.

Chirkinian, aware of Longhurst's habits, worried that Henry wouldn't be able to climb the 16th tower, but he always found a way, and he was quite agile, I must say. He did his job magnificently. My favorite Longhurst line, which I borrowed many times—the most memorable occasion being when Mark O'Meara, tied with David Duval and Fred Couples, lined up a birdie putt on the 72nd green to win the 1998 Masters—was very simple: "I guess there's nothing more to do now than just watch." Said Chirkinian: "Anyone open their mouth, and I'll kill 'em." Whitaker, whom I worked with on the CBS Golf Classic, was equally gifted. Without cue cards, he consistently delivered the most poignant essays. He was able to get in and get out, the true secret to good television.

Any review of my career in the business must revolve around The Masters, the most heavily watched telecast in the game year after year. I feel tremendously blessed to have worked for the network that has covered the tournament every year since 1956. Not many remember what you say at the normal tour event, but everybody remembers what you say at The Masters. Say the wrong thing—i.e., McCord, Whitaker—and you probably won't be saying *anything* when the azaleas bloom the following spring. That was no problem for me. I just talked golf.

The pressure started before the tournament did. A rehearsal wasn't just a rehearsal. It felt like a live show. Augusta National placed committee members in the production truck to make sure we were giving the tournament its proper respect. There was nothing to worry about. With all the prestige CBS received from covering The Masters, we weren't about to be stricken with a sudden case of irreverence. Nobody fooled around.

Though the 13th hole became my familiar spot, I started at the less glamorous 14th—only fitting, I suppose, with 14 being the hole I 3-putted in 1956, 1958, and 1960. Maybe now, from a higher vantage point, I'd be able to read the green. I also spent some time on the ground, though it took a little convincing. Cliff Roberts, at first, wasn't too crazy about the idea, and when Cliff wasn't crazy about an idea, the idea usually died. He was concerned that the presence of a TV commentator on the fairways might be too intrusive. "Frank Chirkinian wants you to go on the ground for the playoff," Roberts said. "What kind of questions would you ask the players?"

Questions? "Mr. Roberts, if you put that microphone in front of my face when I'm in a Masters playoff," I told him, "I'd hit you over the head with it. I do not ask questions."

I think that was the right answer.

"Frank," Roberts said, "you may put Ken on the ground."

My most memorable on-ground experience came in 1987, the year Larry Mize sank his famous chip at 11—the second playoff hole—to outduel Greg Norman. The shout heard on the air came from me. I couldn't believe the ball went in. Nor, I imagine, could Norman.

Any mention of Norman stirs memories of Masters collapses, a subject I know all too well. The first collapse I covered for CBS was in 1979, the poor victim being Ed Sneed, who bogeyed the last three holes and then lost in a sudden-death playoff with Fuzzy Zoeller, the eventual winner, and Tom Watson. After Sneed bogeyed 16, Chirkinian told me to go to the 10th tee in case of a playoff. "Frank, are you kidding?" I said. "No way. Let me just watch 17." One bogey later, I said: "Frank, I'm on my way." Coincidentally, I gave Sneed a few lessons on pitching earlier in the week, which he utilized quite well during the final round, hitting wonderful shots that led to birdies at 13 and 15. When he emerged from Butler Cabin, I felt the need to console him. Just like I had been consoled 23 years earlier.

"You did yourself proud," I told him. "I'm so sorry."

To be more honest, I think I was, in a way, also consoling myself. Watching him stumble down the stretch brought the disappointment of 1956 back to the surface all over again. I suppose it was never really far away, in any case. But I'm luckier than Sneed. I have 1964 to cheer me up. He doesn't. All he has is 1979. He wrote me a very warm letter thanking me for my help.

Six years later, it was Curtis Strange's turn to lose The Masters. For Strange, everything didn't fall apart tortuously, piece by piece. Instead, he lost it with one shot, a shot he should never have tried in the first place. At 13, I was in my usual seat when Strange, leading the tournament, hit his drive safely in the fairway, about 210 yards from the green. He took an iron out of his bag to lay up and avoid Rae's Creek. (If only Palmer had done that in 1958!)

"He can still make four, but the worst he'll make is five," I said. "Even though he could possibly reach the green, it's a smart move."

Well, it would have been a smart move.

"Wait a minute. Now, we're going into another dimension." I said, as Strange changed his mind and took off the head cover to a fairway wood. I could hear Chirkinian on my headset, saying, "Run with it," and so I did. "We're now putting three, four, five, six, and seven into the equation. I believe this is a bad move and could be a mental error."

Sure enough, Strange's ball finished in Rae's Creek, leading to a most unnecessary bogey. Strange found the water again at 15 and lost by two to Bernhard Langer. It cost him the chance to be the first player in many years to win a major after posting an 80 or higher on his scorecard. (The next year, during the week of the Doral tournament, Strange confronted me in the locker room. "I want to tell you something," he said. "If I had to do it all over again, I would still take the wood out." I wasn't intimidated. "That's fine, Curtis," I replied, "and you'd still lose again." I walked off without waiting for his answer. I hear now he has said the wood was the wrong play.)

Then, of course, there was Norman, who deserves the most empathy. He owns everything except a green jacket. He once asked Chirkinian, his good friend, how he could learn to win again.

"Ask Venturi," Chirkinian said. "He'll tell you how to win again."

Norman asked me and I told him.

"Sell your jet, sell your yacht, sell your motorcycles and sports cars," I said. "Go live in a Motel 6 and eat hamburgers, and you'll get hungry again. You're not hungry enough." He laughed and so did I.

Norman's first heartbreaker at Augusta in 1986 was of course overshadowed by the historic Jack Nicklaus charge on the back nine. Missing the green as poorly as Norman did with his 4-iron approach at the 72nd hole was almost impossible to comprehend. If he put his practice bag down, he couldn't do that again. (I believe, incidentally, that Nicklaus should have retired right then, or at least, scaled back to only a few events. Nobody in sports could ever retire in more dramatic fashion.)

Norman's 1987 loss to Larry Mize was easier to understand. What can you do when your opponent hits a shot like that? Of course, 1996 was the toughest of them all. I remember seeing

Norman on the driving range on the morning of Sunday's final round. He appeared a little nervous. The downfall, I believe, started at the 9th hole, when he made the one mistake you can't make on that green, hitting it short. The ball rolled off the green and back down the hill, leading to a bogey. He suddenly looked like a defeated player. For me, the round was very tough to watch; the similarities with 1956 were almost eerie. Yet there was no time for self-pity. I had a job to do.

Chirkinian, recognizing the parallel, told everyone to let me run with it, and I did, describing Norman's frame of mind while everything was falling apart. Afterward, Norman told me: "You got into my brain." He seemed surprised. Greg, I reminded him, I've been there. The players weren't the only ones to make costly mistakes at Augusta. While I never said anything that landed me in hot water—I suppose the place had already caused me enough heartache—a few others weren't spared.

In 1966, two years before I joined CBS, Jack Whitaker was working the 18-hole playoff between Jack Nicklaus, Tommy Jacobs, and Gay Brewer Jr. Because it was a Monday, there were a lot of first-timers in the gallery, using passes from the longtime ticket holders who couldn't attend. To put it mildly, these newcomers got a little carried away with their good fortune. Whitaker didn't put it so mildly, saying as they charged toward the 18th green, breaking through the ropes and running past the Masters security: "It's a mob scene." Frankly, I remember the scene and, guess what, it *was* a mob scene! There wasn't any better way to describe it. But accurate or not, that image wasn't one that Cliff Roberts wanted to be portrayed to the rest of the nation. Whitaker would not do another Masters telecast until the early seventies, and only then because Longhurst became ill during the week of the tournament.

Of course the other and more well-documented Masters gaffe was committed at the 1994 Masters by Gary McCord. I was in the 13th tower when I heard McCord make his infamous "body bags" comment—he was referring to the fact that if you hit it over the 17th green at Augusta, you're basically dead in terms of being able to save par. Right away, I looked at my cameraman and my spotter, and we all knew this was going to be trouble. The language McCord used wasn't golf lingo. He could just as easily have said what has been said so many times before: that "If you knock it over this [the 17th] green, you're dead; you have no chance." (I knew from firsthand experience. My approach shot on the final day in 1956 had hit the green and rolled down the hill. I bogeyed.) McCord made another inappropriate comment—this time about "bikini wax"—when referring to the speed of the greens. I was sure Chirkinian was going to hear something from the club.

I felt sorry for McCord. His material may have been able to pass at other tournaments, but not at Augusta. Over the years, McCord chose not to seek forgiveness. All he would have had to say was something like, "I miss The Masters. I made a simple mistake. I thought it was funny, but it was wrong," and he would have been asked back.

What happened to McCord pales in comparison to the fate suffered by another colleague, Ben Wright, one of the most talented commentators the game has ever known. McCord lost a week. Ben lost a career. I felt very sorry for him. From the start, when his interview with the Wilmington, Delaware, reporter was originally published in the spring of 1995, Ben should have come clean, admitting that he, indeed, made some inappropriate remarks about lesbians on the LPGA Tour and how some women's breasts interfere with their golf swing. If he had, I'm convinced the whole matter would have blown away rather quickly. The media would have gone scouting for another victim. Once it came out, however, that he had lied in his initial denial, CBS made the decision to terminate his contract.

Nonetheless, I have always believed that Ben's punishment was too severe. One year off the air would have been more than sufficient. Take what happened to Marv Albert. The controversy he was involved in in 1997 made Ben look like Mary Poppins, and yet he was back on NBC in almost no time. I've only spoken to Ben once in the past few years. I miss our friendship.

Soon after the Ben Wright dismissal, CBS parted with another valuable resource, Frank Chirkinian. What happened to Chirkinian confirmed once again the first rule about the television business: everyone is expendable.

What was Chirkinian's big crime? There was none. All he did, according to my sources, was refuse to hire Pat Summerall, the former CBS golf anchor, who wanted to do The Masters again. Summerall, however, was working for Fox, which had taken football away from CBS. The problem was that Summerall was good friends with Jack Stephens, The Masters chairman. I never found out what Summerall said to him, though I suspect CBS soon got word that Stephens didn't want Chirkinian to do the tournament anymore. He would be free to do the rest of the schedule, but without The Masters, it would mean nothing.

I was very angry. I would have been nowhere without Frank Chirkinian standing up for me. He gave me a chance when I was running out of them. Now it was time for me to stand up for him. I spoke with the president of CBS Sports in an attempt to save Chirkinian's job.

"You're making a big mistake," I told him. "He is the man, the best in all TV. He's the one who started it all."

I was talking to a deaf ear. The way he was nodding his head, it was obvious it was a done deal. Chirkinian was replaced by his longtime assistant, Lance Barrow, a former spotter for Summerall in football. I got along with Barrow, who has done a solid job, but it wasn't the same at CBS without Chirkinian.

My favorite television experience didn't come at The Masters or during any other golf tournament. It resulted from a simple conversation between me and an old friend. His name was Ben Hogan. Hogan didn't do interviews, as everyone knew. He preferred a quiet existence, hitting balls at Shady Oaks and having lunch at the roundtable overlooking the 18th green. But in 1983, in anticipation of the network's annual visit to cover the Colonial tournament, Chirkinian figured he might as well give it a try. To many people's surprise, Hogan said yes, on two conditions.

First, he wanted us to make it appear that the meeting was casual. He didn't want other networks to get the idea that he was available for interviews at any given moment. Second, only I could do the interview. Hogan didn't trust many people, but he did trust me. CBS asked him what issues he might like to address. He didn't suggest any. All he said was, "Whatever Ken Venturi wants to ask me." I was very flattered.

We did the interview at Shady Oaks. I asked the first question from my notes, but I didn't look down again. I couldn't. Hogan didn't take his eyes off me. He was on a roll, displaying a vulnerability that many didn't know he possessed. Especially moving was when he reflected about the time he went to play a tournament in Oakland, California. He was almost out of money and hope. And if that weren't daunting enough, one morning that week he was without wheels. Someone stole all four tires off his car. But Hogan, being Hogan, persevered, winning the most important check of his life, $285, the check that made so many others possible. While he told this amazing story, I saw tears in his eyes. I had never seen tears in Ben Hogan's eyes. When the cameras stopped rolling, Hogan and I, along with tour players John Cook and Tom Byrum, hung around to hear some more stories. I know those guys will never forget that day and neither will I.

The interview, aired during the Colonial tournament, generated very positive reviews, though not from everyone. One TV critic complained we didn't ask Hogan the really tough questions. His idea of a tough question, for instance, was: why don't you play the Senior Tour? Tough? More like stupid. Hogan couldn't walk a full 18 holes, and, as a traditionalist, he wasn't going to use a cart. There was no need to ask him about it. The "expert" also mentioned that we should have talked about Hogan's antagonistic relationship with the press. My opinion was that the only people who cared about how Hogan got along with the press were the press.

The TV critic wasn't the first to be way off base, and he wouldn't be the last. I learned long ago not to pay too much attention to them. Most of the time, they are guilty of the same crime: ignorance. When I read their stories about the proper way to play a particular shot at Augusta, it made me laugh. Excuse me, I felt like saying, but I don't seem to recall you ever playing in The Masters.

The critics were on my case for years, suggesting I was too kind to the players. If that's the charge, I can enter only one plea: guilty. They always wanted me to be more like Johnny Miller, but, believe me, that was never going to happen. I think Johnny is a smart guy, but a little too harsh for my taste. I treated every player the way I would have wanted them to treat me. I would never have used the word stupid, for instance, in reference to Jean Van de Velde's famous blunder at the 1999 British Open. (Van de Velde enjoyed a seemingly comfortable three-stroke lead entering the final hole, but then teed off with a driver instead of using an iron, which would have been the much safer choice. He finished the hole with a triple bogey, then lost in a three-man playoff.) Even though it *was* stupid, I would have described it as "a complete mental breakdown," perhaps the worst I had ever seen, but I would never go further than that. The player knows when he's made a stupid move, and so does the viewer at home. I would have stated the obvious.

The critics also accused me of being too much of a cheerleader. Again, guilty as charged. Even Chirkinian would remind me about it. "Watch yourself," he said if I went too far, which I did on occasion with John Cook and a few other of my favorite players. A clear indication was when my voice got higher. "You're starting to root," Chirkinian said.

There were times when it was impossible not to root. We're "objective" broadcasters, I suppose, but we're also human beings, and, besides, we're not covering the Mideast peace talks here. This is a game, and we should always remember that.

Exhibit A: Ben Crenshaw in 1995, winning The Masters days after he lost his mentor, Harvey Penick. Anyone who wasn't rooting for Crenshaw didn't have a heart. The line I remember from that day was when Crenshaw's hooked tee shot at the 14th hole bounced off a tree back into the fairway. "I guess Harvey Penick is in the gallery," I said. (I had a nice chat with Ben just before the tournament. "I can't break 80," he told me. "What the hell is the difference?" I said. "Play this one for Harvey. Talk to him while you're walking around." Crenshaw called a month or so after the tournament to thank me for my support.)

Exhibit B: In 2001, at the International tournament in Colorado, I was rooting for Tom Pernice Jr., who prevailed. I'll never forget when his daughter, born with a disease that causes blindness, touched his face. I couldn't speak.

My most formidable challenge in the booth, from the beginning, was to control the stammering. Over the years, I was much better in one-on-one conversations, but television, with its numerous distractions, was much tougher.

The way I coped with it was to keep my thoughts as far ahead of my words as possible. Therefore, if I knew I was approaching a word that was likely to give me trouble, there was time to think of an alternative. Sometimes, my grammar and phrasing would be a bit awkward, but I was able to make my point. I still have difficulty on the telephone. If I'm doing an interview, I close the blinds and try to visualize the face of the person on the other end of the line.

I was often asked why I didn't try to announce other sports besides golf. The answer was always the same one I first told baseball pitcher Don Drysdale many years ago. On a golf course, I know what I'm talking about. I've never pitched the seventh game of the World Series.

When I reflect back on my time with CBS, there is one individual, in addition to Frank Chirkinian, to whom I owe so much, Jim Nantz. I can't imagine what my last 17 years would have been like without Jim, whom I love like a son.

We became friends during the 1986 Masters. From the start, we formed a special bond that went far beyond the work environment. Jim possesses amazing recall, pulling statistics and anecdotes out at the most opportune moments. I was the exact opposite, which is why we complemented each other so well. I didn't spend a moment doing any research about a player's background. I wasn't interested in whether he was having trouble with a wife or trouble with a caddie. All I focused on was what he was doing in the tournament. During my final telecast, the fourth round of the 2002 Kemper tournament, I was especially moved by Jimmy's comments. I was holding up pretty well emotionally, but when I looked into his eyes, I saw the same expression I saw in 1964 when Ray Floyd picked my ball out of the final hole. I lost it again.

Could I have worked at CBS for another two or three years? Perhaps. I was offered a pretty sweet contract by network president Leslie Moonves. But, to me, timing has always been important. I learned that from Joe DiMaggio a long time ago. We were having dinner one night a few years after he retired.

"Joe, you had some good years left," I told him. "Why did you retire?"

"Ken, I want you to remember this," he said. "When you're good, you can always get in. It's knowing when to get out."

I knew when to get out.

People want to know what I think of today's golf coverage. No longer on the CBS payroll, I can tell them. Generally, not much. The one problem I see over and over on all the networks is commentators talking over golf shots. A lot of times, they're even discussing a different player. Chirkinian would have had a coronary if that happened on one of his telecasts.

"One of the rules," he told me, "is never talk over a golf shot."

He believed in the premise: golf shot, golf shot, golf shot. Today's coverage has veered too far away from that premise. The commentators have also gone out of control with swing analysis. Often, what they point out is not accurate. I wonder how many viewers have developed poor mechanics because of something they picked up on television.

I'm not sure what the future holds, but I do know that it wouldn't hurt to learn a couple of things from the past. One would be the need for perspective. Jack Whitaker was brilliant in this area, and so was longtime ABC host Jim McKay. More than any other sport, golf, with its unique blend of fortitude and fortune, lends itself so well to reflection, to a look at how human beings hold up in the most adverse conditions. The key is to provide poignant essays without interfering with the action, which, I believe, can be done. The commentators also have to do a better job with interviews. They don't ask questions. They issue statements: "You hit that 5 iron pretty well at 14, curving it around the pond, getting it on the proper level of the green, didn't you?" "Yes," the player says. Wow, what a revealing answer! What is so hard, I wonder, about asking a simple question, such as: "What were you trying to do at 14?"

I don't want to be perceived as one of those former announcers who acts like he knows everything. Perhaps I'm already too late. I do know that I care very deeply about these issues. I spent 35 years in the business.

There are many things I miss: I miss the back nine on Sunday. I miss David Feherty's wit. I miss Jim Nantz's sensitivity. I miss the cameramen, the spotters, the statisticians, and all the talented people who don't get their mugs on TV.

I miss the 13th hole at Augusta.

Chapter Seventeen

GOOD-BYE TO BEAU, BEN, AND GENE

In late 1996, Beau started to have headaches. We weren't overly concerned at first, but when they started getting worse, we went to Dr. John Little in Naples. Beau had been through tough times before, contracting breast cancer back in the late seventies and cancer of the lymph nodes during the eighties. For a little thing, she was quite a warrior.

The results of the biopsy, as we feared, were not good. The doctor suggested they go in right away. They were able to remove part of the tumor in the brain but couldn't be certain that they caught everything. He wanted to take another biopsy, but the timing was wrong. Beau was determined to accompany me on our usual trip in April to Augusta and Hilton Head. She loved those places, and, looking back, I think she sensed this would be her last chance. During much of the drive from South Carolina to Marco Island, she slept in the van. I kept stealing glances, worried about my girl.

When we returned, she went in for the other biopsy. The news was worse than ever. They discovered five more tumors, all inoperable. Beau asked Dr. Little to keep the truth from me, but I knew him pretty well from the back surgeries he had performed on me and Gene Sarazen. I asked him the most difficult question I ever asked anyone: how long? July 15, give or take a few days, he estimated.

I was devastated. What do you do when you find out your soul mate, the only woman you have ever truly loved, has three months to live? What do you talk about? You try, I suppose, to do what we did—to go on as normally as possible. But it was all such an act. Normal, whatever that meant, would never be possible again, and we both knew it. We never did have a big talk about death but, with the looks we gave each other, the hugs, the kisses, the tears, we were saying our good-byes every moment of every day.

I wanted to stay home during those three months, but Beau wouldn't hear of it. She told me to be where I belonged: in the 18th tower. She didn't want to feel that she was holding me back—typical Beau, dying, yet thinking of someone else. I went, but I called her during most commercial breaks. Even that wasn't frequent enough, so I devised a special code to communicate with her over the air. If I touched my left eyebrow or my right ear, I was telling her that I loved her. I transmitted so many signals the first day that Jim Nantz thought I was trying to tell him he had a mark on his face. Thank God for hospice care. The people who watched over Beau 24 hours a day made her as peaceful as possible.

In June, I went to Congressional Country Club to do an interview just before the U.S. Open, the first Open there since my triumph in 1964. I usually returned once a year, when I was in Washington to cover the Kemper tournament for CBS. (In 1980, the first time the Kemper was played at Congressional, when John Mahaffey won, I was on the 18th fairway when I heard a loud roar. Assuming it was for Mahaffey, who was approaching the green, I stopped talking. Little did I know that the ovation was for me. "Hey, you stupid s.o.b.," Chirkinian finally said into my earpiece. "That applause is for you." Even Mahaffey was applauding. I became very emotional, but, remembering I was there to do a job, I quickly got out of the way.)

When I went back, I was always excited to see everyone, especially my old caddie, William Ward. I would hit a few balls and joke with him about how he felt when I picked his name out of the hat.

That brief visit in 1997 was different. William was dead and Beau was dying. I wasn't in the mood to celebrate. I also still disagreed with the USGA's decision to make the finishing hole a par-3. As a strong traditionalist, I believed the winner should take the same victory walk I had taken. I stayed just long enough to see a few people and then rushed home to be with Beau.

A few weeks later, on July 3, I was supposed to go out for dinner. Something told me to stay home. I was reading a book in the family room when my dog, Geoff, a yellow Labrador, kept walking back and forth to the bedroom.

Finally, he came in and put his paws all over me, biting and pulling on my leg. "Stop it, Geoff," I kept saying. But he persisted, taking a few steps toward the bedroom where Beau was sleeping. I finally decided to follow. He looked back several times to make sure I was coming. When I reached the bedroom, I found out why he was so persistent. He put his paws on the bed and touched her hand.

Beau opened her eyes, looking at me. I cradled her, while I gave her a kiss on the forehead. She looked up, blinked, and died in my arms. If it weren't for Geoff, I never would have seen Beau alive for one last time.

So many people called or wrote to express their condolences. I was especially touched by one call from Texas.

"I'm so sorry, Ken," said Valerie Hogan. "I don't know what I would do if I lost Ben."

Her call reminded me of the time, in 1973, when Beau and I ran into Hogan and his wife at the "21" Club in New York.

"Beau, Henny Bogan," Hogan said, meeting her for the first time. "I always thought Ken would have a little bit of brains. He finally showed me he had some when he married a girl from Fort Worth."

Soon the calls stopped coming. Everything became quiet—too quiet. Those moments were the saddest. Beau meant the world to me, more than I ever realized. And now my world was gone.

I knew one thing. I wasn't prepared to sit at home on Marco Island and spend the rest of my days playing cards at the club. With a little push from Jim Nantz, I signed on for another three years at CBS. I would be surrounded by good friends and the game I loved. Golf was my salvation before, and it would be my salvation again.

But on July 25, only three weeks after losing Beau, I lost someone else close to me. I was in Hartford, Connecticut, preparing for coverage of the Greater Hartford Open, when I heard the news. Ben Hogan was dead.

That afternoon, I spoke to Valerie. She told me not to worry about making it to the funeral, with it being so soon since Beau's death. When I told her I would be there, she asked if I would be one of the honorary pallbearers. "You were Ben's first choice," she said. The following Tuesday, I sat in the back of the church. The memories rushed to the surface:

- *1954, our first round together at The Masters, when he told me to call him Ben—"Serves me right for looking into an amateur's bag."*
- *1956, the match with Byron Nelson and Harvie Ward at Cypress Point—"I'm not about to be tied by a couple of amateurs."*
- *1958, when I waited to hear from him before signing with U.S. Royal—"You will always play with me."*
- *1966, the exchange on the second green at The Olympic Club— "Who gives a shit? You've beaten people long enough."*

There are so many more memories. When Hogan and I practiced together, he asked me first where I wanted to hit balls. After I picked out a spot, he always set up behind me. One day, I told him that I figured out why he did that. "You want to know when I'm watching you, but you don't want me to know when you're watching me," I said. He smiled.

My favorite Hogan story was when he and I were playing Seminole in preparation for the 1958 Masters. Hogan was trying to decide which 4 wood he would use in the tournament.

"I'll take the one you don't want," I told him, "because I really need one for Augusta."

On the Wednesday before the tournament, while playing a practice round at Augusta, Hogan suddenly paused at the 13th hole.

"Kenny, come over here for a minute," he said.

"What can I do for you, Ben?" I said.

"I've got to make a decision," he said. "Which one of these 4 woods do *you* like best?"

I needed to quickly figure out a way to outfox him. I knew that if I were to pick the one I wanted, I wouldn't get it.

"I like this one," I said, pointing to the 4 wood that I liked less.

"So do I," said Hogan, predictably, handing me the other one. Mission accomplished. I outfoxed Hogan, not an easy thing to do.

Years later, I finally came clean.

"I still got the best one," he insisted.

Actually, I still have the best one, which I keep in my office.

I learned so much from Hogan. More than anything else, I learned how to compete. He always said: "There's three ways to beat somebody. You outwork them, you outthink them, and then you intimidate them."

He was a master at intimidation, even better than Jack Nicklaus or Tiger Woods. "When you walk on the first tee, you don't say, 'Good luck.'" Hogan told me. "You look them straight in the eye and if the other players say good luck, you say, 'you too.' 'You too' can mean almost anything."

One day, Hogan and I were playing with another touring pro. In a shrill voice, the golfer said, "Have a good time, Ben, and play well." All Hogan said was "thank you." The player had no chance.

Beau was an amazing giver. Name the cause, and she was doing something to support it.

"How was your day?" I would often ask her.

"Oh, I helped some people," she said. She usually didn't provide details, but I could tell the satisfaction she derived. One of her favorite causes was the plight of abused women and children. When Beau died, I made it one of my favorite causes. I have absolutely no sympathy for anybody who harms a woman or child. I don't consider myself a violent man, but I don't want to think about what I would do to them if I had the chance.

I started to raise money to help build a shelter in the Naples area for abused women and children. My strongest desire was that the shelter would fill as few rooms as possible. I was a little hesitant. The same people are always asked for money, and I knew that every charity is important. I went ahead. I knew Beau wouldn't hesitate.

Starting in the summer of 1998, I approached tour players to see if they would participate in an outing to raise money. I was hopeful, if pessimistic. I hated to be so cynical, but getting pros, with all the money on the table these days, to show up for free, not even paid expenses, would be a difficult chore.

I was wrong. Almost instantly, three big names—Greg Norman, Mark O'Meara, and Nick Price—committed. In all, 23 players showed up on March 8, 1999, at Eagle Creek Country Club in Naples, the day after the Doral tournament. They included Tom Kite, Ben Crenshaw, David Duval, Ernie Els, Stuart Appleby, and Tom Watson, just to name a few. Fred Couples and Jack Nicklaus couldn't make it but sent donations. We raised $900,000, the first step toward the $6.5 million we needed to begin construction. Outback Steakhouse catered the event at no charge, while Anheuser-Busch provided beverages.

I was touched by the support of Jim Nantz, who served as host, and Gene Sarazen, who made the entire day extra special.

Sarazen, 97 years young, signed autographs and shook hands on the first tee. He was as funny as ever. When he was introduced to Els, Sarazen rose from his chair and immediately brought up a sensitive subject. At Doral, Els' chip shot on the final hole failed to reach the putting surface, costing him a chance to win the tournament.

"I've always wanted to meet somebody who flubbed a $500,000 chip shot," he said to Els.

Els turned completely red. The moment was hysterical, though I don't believe Ernie was one of the people laughing.

With the assistance of Florida governor Jeb Bush and some extremely generous anonymous donors, we raised the funds for the shelter. In late 2002, the 35,000-square-foot shelter, christened "The Beau Venturi Home: The Wings of Hope," officially opened. The place is remarkable, with enough room, believe it or not, for a kennel where the kids can bring their animals. I was quite moved. For the longest time, I wondered why God took Beau away from me. I now had my answer.

"Without Beau," I said to the crowd assembled on the day we opened the doors, "there would be no Beau Venturi Home. God took her life so that she could save so many others."

God saved mine, that's for sure. On the day I prayed in the basement, way back in 1964, he gave me one more chance. But while I promised that I would find a way to "give back," it wasn't until I met Beau that I learned what giving back was all about.

The first issue to seize my attention was the one that played such a huge role in my upbringing—stammering. For as long as I could remember, I did everything to hide it. Better, I figured, for people to think I was arrogant than to make fun of me. But in the seventies, I stopped hiding and started helping. I wanted to show youngsters that they could learn to deal with it, just like I did.

I joined the board of the Stuttering Foundation of America, speaking in public about the problem as often as possible. I tell them that some very prominent people in history, such as Winston Churchill, Marilyn Monroe, Bruce Willis, and James Earl Jones, have overcome it. When they meet me, they can't believe that I was one of *them*. I'm still one of them. Once, at a children's clinic, I met a father who was very ashamed of his son. I, in turn, was very ashamed of the father.

"It's really embarrassing," he told me. "I can't have a conversation with him."

The guy was making me angry. I couldn't hold back.

"Do you know what you're saying?" I asked him. "I'm a stammerer. I stammered just like your son when I was 11 years old. I couldn't say my own name. Did you ever say you loved your son?"

"No," he said, remarkably.

"I want you to go into the next room," I said, "and tell your son that you are sorry for everything you've done and that you didn't understand what he was going through. Give him a hug and tell him that you love him very much."

The father did what I asked.

"I love you too, Dad," the son replied. It was his first complete sentence.

Another cause that has meant a lot to me is Guiding Eyes for the Blind. My involvement was due to the efforts of Charlie Boswell, whom I met during the 1954 Masters. Boswell, a captain in World War II, lost his sight saving three young soldiers from a burning tank. One of them was responsible, in turn, for returning

Boswell to safety. People like Charlie Boswell make me proud to be an American.

When the organization was having trouble raising money in the late seventies, Boswell approached me. I couldn't say no. I'm proud to say that, through my fund-raising efforts, which includes an annual golf tournament, I have been responsible for putting 350 dogs in the hands of blind people at no charge. The average cost of each dog is currently about $25,000. When I worked in the 18th tower, I always tried to keep the blind listeners in my mind, describing details that may have seemed obvious to the viewers.

Giving back also involves giving to the game. For years, I have helped young players, such as John Cook, Steve Elkington, Tom Purtzer, and others. I would never take any money. How could I, after all the free lessons I received from Byron Nelson and Ben Hogan? My only condition was that they couldn't tell people about it. I didn't want to get flooded with phone calls. Even so, a lot of amateurs approached me for lessons. "I got good news and bad news," I would tell them. "The bad news is that it's really going to cost you. The good news is that you can write the check to the charity of my choice."

In May 1999, I was sitting with Jim Nantz and Byron Nelson in the booth at Nelson's tournament in Texas when I received a phone call from Mary Ann Sarazen. Her father, the Squire, was gone. Only two months had passed since he showed up for Beau's outing and one month since he hit the ceremonial tee shot at Augusta.

"Would you do the eulogy?" Mary Ann asked me.

"Mary Ann, there are so many people," I said.

"I know, but dad's last words, before he died, were, 'I want Ken Venturi to do my eulogy.'" End of discussion. I delivered the eulogy.

Once again, sitting in the church, mourning another lost friend, all the memories came back.

I thought back to Augusta National in 1983, when I filled in as one of the honorary starters for Byron Nelson, who had recently lost his wife, Louise. Approaching the tee, I was more nervous than I had been during all the times I played in The Masters or the U.S. Open. I was thinking the same, terrifying thought that occurs to many golfers: don't whiff it! I'm not kidding. Here I was, the "authority" in the game, a major championship winner. If I were to mess up, I would never hear the end of it.

Sarazen teed off first, hitting a solid drive. "You got to get it past Sarazen," I told myself. I did, thank goodness. In fact, I was left with only an 8 iron into the green. In all the years I played that hole, I never had an 8 iron into the green. I made birdie, and went out in 33. Man, I was cooking. Too bad we were scheduled to play only nine holes.

"Let's keep going," I told the Squire, jokingly, of course. "I can lead this tournament."

"Are you crazy?" he said. "We're going in for lunch."

During lunch, he called everyone over.

"Ken could have shot 30 today," he said. "It was the easiest 33 you ever laid your eyes on."

Another Sarazen memory had to do with a round he and I played on Marco Island.

"Mind if I join you?" Sarazen said, as I prepared to tee off with Dean Webb and Terry Diehl, who played on the tour for a few years.

"I'll have to ask those two guys if it's OK," I joked. They almost passed out.

"Then let's have a match," Sarazen said.

"Mr. Sarazen and I will play you two," I said. "How many strokes does Mr. Sarazen get?"

"I don't want any strokes," Sarazen said. "We'll play them even."

We arrived at the 18th hole all square. I knocked it in there about six feet from the pin, while Sarazen must have been at least 45 feet away. Lo and behold, he holed the putt for a birdie.

Webb missed, and I picked up. It was now up to Diehl to halve the match.

While Diehl was lining up his 12-foot putt, I whispered in his ear.

"If you make this putt," I said, "you will never get another lesson as long as you live."

He understood and missed the putt.

Sarazen bought lunch, proceeding to tell stories of his era, many of which included the great Walter Hagen. Finally, Webb and Diehl had to go. We escorted them to the front door. As they left, Sarazen said: "Boys, come back when you can play a little better." That was typical Gene Sarazen.

From Beau's death in 1997 to Sarazen's two years later, I did my share of crying. I didn't realize how empty the world would suddenly become. But, as the new millennium approached, I was excited for the first time in a long time. I would be taking on a challenge I had been dreaming about for years. Little did I know that there would be another challenge awaiting me.

One I never dreamed about.

Chapter Eighteen

WINNING A CUP, AND A LADY

Since the 1965 Ryder Cup, when I was a member of the victorious U.S. squad, I looked forward to one day returning as the captain. But, because of my abbreviated career as a player, I feared that chance would never come. When I made a name for myself in television, I became more hopeful. Maybe, just maybe, this would be the way to receive the honor I so deeply coveted.

In the late eighties, I went from hope to euphoria. The PGA of America asked if I would be interested in leading the team at the matches scheduled for the Belfry in 1989. Interested? I felt the way I did when Byron Nelson asked me to join him for a round at San Francisco Golf Club in 1952. I couldn't reply quickly enough. I was ready. After dominating for so long, the United States had lost two straight matches to the Europeans, in 1985 and 1987. We were determined to put an end to this surprising streak. Though I was in my late fifties, older than other captains, I knew so many of the players from my years in the 18th tower. I knew their games, their personalities, and what pairings would or would not work.

The PGA of America asked me to keep it quiet. Let's wait until a final decision is made, they said.

I waited and waited and waited until one day, I found out that a captain had been named and it wasn't me. The choice was Ray Floyd. I had no problem with what the PGA of America did, but I had a huge problem with how they did it. They never called or wrote me a letter. I felt rejected, reminding me of when I wasn't invited to the 1964 Masters. Only this time I couldn't win a U.S. Open to prove myself.

As the years progressed, I assumed my only opportunity was gone for good. The captains—Dave Stockton (1991), Tom Watson (1993), Lanny Wadkins (1995), Tom Kite (1997)—were all in their forties, while I was over 60.

Then, in early 1999, PGA Tour Commissioner Tim Finchem asked if he could speak to me.

"Would you consider being captain of the [2000] Presidents Cup team?" he asked me.

Was he speaking to me? I wondered.

The commissioner went on. "I want to make a good push to get you. I think you would be a great captain."

I was so happy I almost hugged the man. He then asked me to keep quiet. Sound familiar?

"Commissioner," I said, "I know I can keep it a secret, but you've got a lot of people."

I kept it a secret, all right, for several months, telling only Jim Nantz and my son Matt. During that time, Finchem called back to tell me it was a done deal but said to wait until they could make the formal announcement. I wasn't going to get robbed this time.

In April, at The Masters, I asked Paul Marchand to be my assistant captain. Marchand was a teammate of Nantz's on the

University of Houston golf team in the late seventies, and was head pro at Houston Country Club. He accepted the assignment.

Finally, in May, my selection as captain was made official. I was free to tell the whole world, which I think I did. I was so excited, though I kept reminding myself that the competition was still more than a year away. There would be plenty of time to get excited later.

I couldn't have asked for a more ideal setup. For starters, the event would be held at the Robert Trent Jones Golf Club in Virginia, only about 40 minutes from Congressional. I felt a certain magic in that part of the country. Second, I would have a chance to make up for what happened at the last Presidents Cup in December 1998, when the U.S. team, led by captain Jack Nicklaus, fell to the International squad, 20$\frac{1}{2}$ to 11$\frac{1}{2}$, at Royal Melbourne Golf Club in Australia. The loss became known as "The Blunder Down Under." I was at Melbourne for CBS. It was a blunder, all right. The United States definitely had something to prove this time around, and I've always loved having something to prove.

In the summer of 2000, as Tiger Woods seized everyone's attention with his dominating performances at the U.S. Open and British Open, I was keeping track to see who would make up my team. Along with Woods, the automatics appeared to be Phil Mickelson, David Duval, Davis Love III, Hal Sutton, Tom Lehman, and Jim Furyk—a pretty talented group, to be sure. After the PGA, won by Woods, the others to get in on points were Notah Begay, Stewart Cink, and Kirk Triplett. Finally, it was up to me to make the two captain's picks, one of my most important decisions.

I wanted so much to pick Couples, the hero from the 1996 matches. But, from the beginning, I told him I wasn't just going to hand it to him. He needed to earn it.

"Get off your ass," I had told him a few months earlier. "I can't pick you if you're going to sit down. You're a natural, a match play man. I could pair you with anyone."

Unfortunately, Couples didn't play nearly enough or well enough. I can't think of any player in recent years who has possessed more innate talent than him. Give me his length and my experience, and it would have been, get off the streets, boys, I'm coming through.

I considered several possibilities, including Justin Leonard, who made the winning putt in the Ryder Cup at Brookline; David Toms; and Chris Perry. But ultimately I picked Loren Roberts, who was in the top 10 until Begay passed him at the PGA, and Paul Azinger. I must admit Azinger, who wasn't even in the top 20 on the points list, was a sentimental choice. He beat cancer, and I guess I had a soft spot for comeback stories. I also felt this could be his last hurrah. With the team firmly in place, I could finally concentrate on potential pairings and other details.

Or so I thought. A few days later, when I went to the doctor in Naples for a routine physical, they discovered that my PSA (prostate specific antigen) count was extremely high. I was in the early stages of prostate cancer.

I would now face another tough decision, one with a lot more at stake than a golf match. Among the options discussed by the physicians in Florida were radiation and surgery. But I knew of another option, proton treatments at the Loma Linda Proton Treatment Center. That would have to wait, however. I took pills to put the cancer in remission that would last for six months. The one thing I wasn't going to do was become a distraction to the team or the event. I kept my news a secret, telling only Jim Nantz and a few close friends.

In mid-October we were ready to play. I thought the week would never arrive. I wanted to win this Cup more than anything. I wanted to go out on top, and I wanted to show the younger players the type of competitor I could be. They knew me only as the golf analyst for CBS, not as the tour professional with the white linen cap.

On the Saturday before the competition, I was honored at the Robert Trent Jones Golf Club, the first gathering in what promised to be an unforgettable experience. I had planned to talk about the game and what it has meant to me. But world events forced me to change my plans. Only days earlier, 17 American soldiers were killed in the bombing of the USS *Cole* in Yemen, a precursor, we all later discovered, to another terrorist attack a year later.

"I want to win more than anything else in the world," I said, "but how important is it, really, when you think about priorities? I would give up anything right now to bring back those 17 young men and women. My players don't know it yet, but I am going to dedicate this week to those young men and women. We're going to wear black ribbons in their honor." We weren't the only ones. When the International team heard about it, they said they would wear the ribbons as well. I was very moved.

I wasn't, however, about to let any politics interfere with my team's preparation. We were scheduled to have dinner in the city with President Clinton, but the White House wanted to set it up for Wednesday, the night before the first day of competition. To me, that was unacceptable. Wednesday night was going to be for ourselves to prepare for the matches.

"Am I the captain?" I asked Commissioner Finchem.

"Yes," he said.

"Then," I said emphatically, "my team will not be going."

I wasn't worried about missing a visit with the president. I missed LBJ in 1964, and I was prepared to miss Bill Clinton in 2000. The White House, realizing I wasn't going to change my mind, rescheduled the dinner for Tuesday night. The evening went well. I know I should probably recall something Knute Rockne–esque that the commander in chief said, but I was already completely focused on the task ahead. I had my game face on. All I lacked was my white cap.

Next up was Wednesday's opening ceremonies. I spoke first, introducing the players one by one. "Last, but not least," I said, "Tiger Woods." I started to sit down when everyone laughed. I looked around and realized I had forgotten to introduce Stewart Cink and Notah Begay. I felt embarrassed, but I quickly recovered. "I want you to know one thing," I said, glancing at Peter Thomson, captain of the International squad. "That's the only mistake I'm going to make all week." Everybody cracked up. That night, we had our team dinner. I could tell the guys were ready.

"We really want to win," said the spirited Hal Sutton, "but we really want to win it for you."

When I woke up the next morning, *I* was ready. The day I dreamed about for years had arrived. I was also sad. The day had arrived without Beau. It didn't feel quite the same. On the way to the first tee, when Marchand, my secretary, Barbara Klimas, and I drove by the 13th tee, we noticed a gorgeous garden with an abundance of white daisies, Beau's favorite flower. I picked a few and put them in our carts, and handed some to Barbara. I returned to the same spot each morning.

"Look over me now," I said to Beau. "I really want this."

She looked over me, all right. We went five for five in the four-some matches on the first day, doing what nobody, not even me, thought was possible. While appreciating the efforts put forth by our main guns, I was most excited over the Cink-Triplett duo, who dispatched Mike Weir and Retief Goosen, 3 and 2. For days, I wasn't sure what I was going to do with Cink and Triplett. With both being rookies in such a pressure-filled event, the logical move would be to pair each of them with a veteran.

So much for logic. I went with a gut feeling, though some people, I heard, had a different gut feeling: Venturi is making a mistake. But I liked the way the two of them related to each other.

"I want you to show these people," I told Cink and Triplett, "that you're as good as I think you are. If you believe that, you'll win."

There was one moment late in that day that I will never forget. While standing near the 18th green, I felt an arm around my neck. I heard a most distinctive voice.

"You no-good s.o.b.," the man said.

"That's the first compliment I've gotten all day," I said.

The voice belonged to Greg Norman, who was with Steve Elkington. They both gave me a hug.

On Friday morning, even with a 5–0 advantage, I was nervous. I had seen too many teams become complacent over the years. I was determined that we weren't going to be one of those teams.

Or maybe we were. In the morning four-ball matches, the International squad captured four of five, slicing the U.S. lead to 6–4. Only a 2 and 1 triumph by Mickelson and Love prevented us from being shut out. Woods and Begay fell to Shigeki Maruyama and Carlos Franco, 3 and 2.

In the afternoon foursomes, we regained our momentum, thanks again to that most unlikely pair—Cink and Triplett, who outdueled Robert Allenby and Stuart Appleby, 2 and 1. The two captain's picks, Loren Roberts and Paul Azinger, cruised to a 5 and 4 victory over Maruyama and Franco. Woods and Begay got back on track, winning the first six holes on the way toward beating Els and Vijay Singh, 6 and 5. We were in control, leading 10 to 5. In five matches, we recorded 26 birdies and one eagle.

On Saturday, the romp continued, as we won four of the five four-ball matches. Cink and Triplett came through again, beating Allenby and Franco, 1 up. As a twosome, they went three for three. Overall, they picked up seven and a half out of a possible eight points (including Cink's 2 and 1 victory in the singles against Greg Norman). I guess they felt they did have something to prove. In any case, with only Sunday's singles remaining, our lead was 14 to 6. All we needed was two and one-half more points, and the Cup would be back in U.S. hands.

Needless to say, I was feeling pretty good about our chances. Yet I was far from content. During our final team get-together on Saturday night I explained why.

"Well, Captain, what's the game plan tomorrow?" said Sutton. "We're going to win."

"Yeah, we're going to win," I acknowledged. "We only have to win three matches out of twelve. But what the hell good is that?"

They gave me strange looks. But I persevered.

"Not all of you were on the team," I said, "but you got the biggest whipping of your life down under two years ago. There are two things I want to do. One, I want to win, and two, I want to break the record." I wasn't concerned, for once, about TV ratings. I wanted there to be no drama at all.

"What would be the incentive?" the team asked.

"I'll tell you about incentive," I said, with former President George Bush sitting next to me. "There's a poster I've always loved. In fact, it was given to me by Frank Sinatra. It shows two buzzards sitting on a dead tree in the middle of the desert. One buzzard turns to the other and says, 'Patience, my ass; let's kill something.'"

The team got the point and became just as determined.

"You got it, buzzard," they said, almost in unison. "We're going to get them."

But getting them wasn't the only goal I had in mind. I wanted to get them the proper way. To be more specific, I didn't want a repeat of Brookline, when the exuberant U.S. players ran onto the 17th green after Justin Leonard made his miraculous birdie putt. I was one of those who thought the celebration was over the top. (Given the situation, I was very proud of how Jose Maria Olazabal behaved. If he somehow had made his putt to halve the hole, it would have been one the greatest putts of all time.)

"That was a response that everybody regrets," I told my squad. "It wasn't planned. But I have a plan this time. We're simply not going to do it. If it's the last putt of the matches, then everyone can run on the green and scream and holler. Only then. Otherwise, no way."

I went to sleep confident we would do the job. The matchups for Sunday's singles, I believed, were definitely in our favor, and that wasn't from sheer luck. There was strategy. Unlike the Ryder

Cup, in which both captains blindly submit the order of players, the Presidents Cup allows more flexibility. In this case, Thomson went first, choosing Robert Allenby. I countered with Paul Azinger, who wanted to lead off so he could play the role of cheerleader. Conveniently, Azinger's game matched up well against Allenby.

I followed with my choice for the second group, and then Thomson countered. The two of us took turns with the first selection in each match.

When he selected Vijay Singh, I responded immediately with Tiger Woods. Hogan would have been proud of that move.

"Oh, damn," Thomson said.

I knew Woods would be motivated to go against Singh. Earlier in the competition, Woods noticed the words *Tiger Who?* stitched on the back of a cap worn by Singh's caddie, Paul Tesori. Woods, I was sure, would show Singh and his caddie *exactly* who he was.

On Sunday, I stopped Woods on the first tee, only a few yards in front of the markers. I grabbed his hand and looked straight into his eyes.

"I want his ass," I told him.

"So do I," he said.

"Enough said," I said, and stepped aside.

We rolled, winning two of the first three matches. As the day went on, each player said the same thing when they saw me: "How is the buzzard doing?"

"He's doing just fine," I said.

In all, we picked up 7 1/2 of the 12 points, including Woods' 2 and 1 victory over Singh. We got the record I wanted, winning 21 1/2 to 10 1/2 when Notah Begay captured the final singles match. No, there weren't any blunders this time, nor any Brookline-type behavior. We carried ourselves with utmost dignity and class, which made me extremely proud.

There was, however, one minor point of contention. Again, it involved the president of the United States. It happened on Saturday. I was informed by my security staff that President Clinton was planning to walk down the fairway with Davis Love III and David Duval, who were playing a four-ball match against Ernie Els and Nick Price.

"No way," I said. "The fairways are for the players, caddies, marshals, and officials. They are crowded enough."

"But it's the president of the United States," a member of the Secret Service said.

"I have my rules," I said.

Former President Bush, who had been around most of the whole week, wouldn't ever think of coming inside the ropes. I also was concerned that Clinton's presence would overshadow my players, who were the day's true stars. My team came first.

I prevailed again. Clinton walked to the ropes and shook hands with Duval and, a few minutes later, Love. He proceeded to cross the fairway with his entourage, went to the motorcade, and left the course. He didn't show up for Sunday's closing ceremonies.

For me, the feeling of fulfillment was more overwhelming than I imagined. I led a U.S. team to victory. A year later, I was approached by a few officials associated with the PGA Tour to see if I had any interest in being the captain for the 2002 Presidents Cup, in South Africa (the matches were postponed a year by the September 11 tragedy).

"After you make a hole in one," I said, "why would you take a mulligan?"

Which, incidentally, also summed up my attitude toward women. Considering how lucky I was to meet Beau, I figured I might as well not even think about meeting anyone else. A miracle like Beau only happens once in a man's life, if that. But on the night of January 17, 2001, I found my second miracle.

I was back in my old stomping grounds, Palm Springs, having just undergone my fourth treatment for prostate cancer. With one major challenge out of the way—the Presidents Cup—I was focusing all my attention on the other. The plan was for me, over a period of three months, to have 39 treatments with protons, which are beamed into your body to kill the cancer. I knew I was in good hands at the Loma Linda Proton Treatment Center, about an hour away from Palm Springs.

On January 17, which was Beau's birthday, I didn't really feel up to doing much, but a friend persuaded me to join him for dinner at a well-known restaurant. When I walked in, I felt like it was 1967 all over again. I saw this beautiful lady in a pink dress serving as the hostess. Her name was Kathleen. She was helping her friend, the owner, until he could find a permanent hostess. I found out later that she had been only minutes away from leaving for the night. Timing, as they say, is everything.

"Man, she is some good-looking lady," I said to the owner.

"Well, let me introduce you," he said.

And so he did. To my amazement, she didn't know my background, which I liked. We talked for a while, listening to Joe Jaggi play Sinatra tunes on the piano. After a while, I asked if she would like to dance.

"You have great rhythm," she told me. "You're a good dancer."

I soon left, but, unlike 1967, I wasn't going to wait a whole year. I wasn't going to wait a whole day. Kathleen and I made plans to have dinner the next night at the same restaurant.

That night, I felt chemistry—the kind of chemistry I was sure I would never feel again. During brunch the following day, she asked what I was doing in town. I told her. I felt like I could tell her anything. She then asked if I would like company on the drive to Loma Linda. I would love it, I told her, and that is when we started to really bond. We engaged in long, wonderful talks, learning everything we could about each other. There were no phones or other distractions. We turned on the CD player and listened to Sinatra, who, I'm sure, would have given his blessing.

At Loma Linda, the hospital staff could not have been more accommodating. They gave me an alias, Ken Vega, so that the press would never catch on that I was there. I also received a key to enter through the back door, and my own room. Kathleen and I made 35 trips together.

Was I afraid? Not really. I took a realistic view. After all I had endured, I once again trusted God would know what to do with me.

Finally, in March, I went through my last treatment.

Both of us were happy and sad. The protons got rid of the cancer. But the PGA Tour was heading back east, which meant I was going home to Marco Island.

I would miss our drives. I would miss our talks. I would miss everything about Kathleen. Yet we were determined that we weren't going to miss our future together. When I returned to Florida, we talked on the phone every night. On the air, I gave her the same signals I gave Beau. By the summer of 2001, we decided that, after my last broadcast with CBS in June 2002, we would share a new home in Rancho Mirage.

Kathleen and I were married in March of 2003 at the Ritz-Carlton in Las Vegas. We invited only a few close friends, with Jim Langley, the head pro at Cypress Point, serving as my best man and witness along with his wife Lou. After champagne and hors d'oeuvres, we were greeted by a gathering of about 300 golfers in the hotel's main ballroom hosted by Jerry Holley, president of All-World Sports, which organizes outings. The golfers were in town for a tournament, where I was being honored. I was thrilled to see so many friends and former colleagues.

After our wonderful time in Las Vegas, we spent a week in San Francisco with my cousins, Barbara and Mario Lombardi, and other family members and friends. I can't believe my luck. I found love a second time, and I wasn't even looking. I finally got my double eagle.

Chapter Nineteen

TRADITION

Every Monday morning, when I read the newspaper, I look
for the articles summarizing the latest PGA Tour event.
And, every Monday morning, I am astounded by the amount of
money the players make. First place brings in close to a million,
a far cry from what a victory was worth when I joined the tour
in 1957. I do not, for a second, begrudge the current players one
single cent. Professional athletes, and that includes golfers, should
receive whatever the forces in the marketplace will bear. Plenty of
people profit from their labor.

Same goes for whatever corporate America decides to give them
in endorsement deals. If the players want to put a logo on every
part of their clothing, which a lot of them do, so be it. It's not for
a traditionalist like me to criticize them. If somebody had offered
me that kind of money, it would've gotten my attention, and, I'm
quite sure, the attention of my peers. I don't blame today's players
for accepting as many opportunities as possible during golf's "silly
season." There are no guarantees. You can be on top of the world
one minute and unable to break 80 the next. Believe me, I know.

At the same time, I worry about the damage the almighty dollar has done and will continue to do in the years ahead. I worry about what it will do to the game we love.

One loss is amateur golf, the cornerstone of the game for so many years. The United States Amateur produced such great champions as Bobby Jones, Harvie Ward, Charlie Coe, Arnold Palmer, and Jack Nicklaus. Nobody lent it more prestige than Jones, who never turned pro. But, except for Tiger Woods, fans would be hard-pressed to cite the tournament's winners in recent decades. In 1956, I came close to winning The Masters. Coe made a similarly strong effort five years later. I don't believe anyone will ever come that close again.

What's the big loss? You may wonder. The big loss is that amateur golf has always reflected the purity of the sport, individuals striving for honor, pride, and achievement, not merely financial reward. Professional golf, with all the money up for grabs, does not possess that same sense of purity. It is a way to make a living— a wonderful living, potentially—but a living, nonetheless.

I truly don't believe that today's players, despite their tremendous talent, are as motivated as they could be. Sure, they want to win, but many seem just as satisfied to earn a sizable check. It wasn't like that in my day, when players, without the security of a six-figure endorsement deal, were hungrier, when winning meant everything. From my vantage point in the 18th tower, I was constantly amazed to see players, two or three shots out of the lead, start to play conservatively down the stretch to protect their position. We never thought about protecting our position. For me and my contemporaries, we felt that if we excelled on the tour, we'd stand a good chance of landing a club pro job. Today, with the kind of money some of these players are making, they could buy the club.

Another loss is the integrity of the classic golf course. Too many—Merion, Cypress Point, Pebble Beach, Riviera, Winged Foot, and others—due to the advances in technology, have become nearly obsolete. One of the most distressing examples is the 13th hole at Augusta National, my home for many years with CBS. The reward is still there, though without nearly as much of the risk. An increasing percentage of the field can reach the green with a solid, not even spectacular, tee shot and a 3 or 4 iron. The hole has almost turned into a long par-4.

Gone, as a result, are the shotmakers, the creative players who have made golf so much fun to watch, the Corey Pavins of the world. Now all you hear about is how a particular player favors a draw or a fade. Ask him to do the opposite, and it might be a problem. Hogan would have been furious. He played practice rounds only with those who could shape a shot properly. If, on a hole where there was a creek to the right of the green and a pin in the right corner, you tried to draw it over the creek, forget it. You'd have to get yourself another game. That wasn't, in his opinion, the way the shot was meant to be played.

So what is my magical new solution? First, it is not so magical or new. I've always been in favor of a uniform golf ball. These days, each company provides a variety of golf balls. You can't hit the ball high? I've got a ball for you. You can't hit the ball low? I've got a ball for you. Can't spin it? No problem. I'm certainly not suggesting that we stop the designing of new clubs and shafts, but you can make a uniform ball for all competitors. Otherwise, when is all this going to stop? And, more important, who is going to be the one to stop it?

When I was on the tour, we basically played the same ball, with only a difference in compression, 90 or 100. If I were commissioner—maybe I should have accepted Joe Dey's offer . . . just kidding!—players would be allowed to use whatever brand they like but the specs would be the same. At each event, the tour would have to consistently sample the golf balls from a dozen or so players to make sure they conformed.

The clubs also need tighter supervision. The decision, which took effect in January 2004, to test "hot" drivers on a voluntary basis is a definite step in the right direction, but only a step. The test needs to be mandatory. While I trust the players, there is no other way to completely remove the cloud of suspicion among the public unless everyone's driver is checked out. Our game, more than any other, can't survive without its integrity fully intact.

Yet another loss is the record books. To me, you might as well throw them all out. How can you possibly compare what Tiger Woods and Ernie Els have accomplished with the exploits of Bobby Jones, Gene Sarazen, Byron Nelson, or Ben Hogan? You can't. Try to imagine what would happen if players today teed off with a hickory shaft and a gutta-percha ball and tried to putt on the unmanicured greens that we often played on. A true roll was rare, indeed. Or if they were forced to hit their approaches from poor fairways, which provided their share of bad lies. One thing is certain: nobody would shoot 31 under par like Ernie Els did in 2003 at the Mercedes Championships in Hawaii.

When I won the American Golf Classic at Firestone in 1964, I believe it was the most proficient week of ball striking in my career. I finished at 5-under 275 and prevailed by five shots. On that course, if you shot a score lower than 280, you were in great position to win. But, in recent years, players have broken 270. Watching that happen to a demanding layout like Firestone is very painful.

These changes are happening too fast. In the fifties and sixties, players seemed to go a whole decade without switching clubs, without constantly searching for the next new Big Whatever. When Byron Nelson gave me a set of irons in 1956, I used them for at least five years. But now, it seems, players are switching almost every month.

The real danger I envision in all this "progress" is that the new clubs have narrowed the gap between the best players in the world and those in the middle of the pack, which keeps the true talents from shining through often enough. No sport, especially golf, thrives when that happens. We want stars. We need stars. Imagine if, because of greater parity, Jack Nicklaus hadn't captured 18 majors or Ben Hogan hadn't won four Opens. The advances in equipment allow players to get by, even win tournaments, with their misses. In my day, a miss meant you could lose 10 or 15 yards. A miss today might be only a few yards.

Technology may, with forceful action, be neutralized. I'm not nearly as optimistic about the other powerful force that has shaped the game in recent years—television. I shouldn't complain, for all the medium did for me and my career. However, I don't like what it's done to some of golf's great traditions.

It was television, I felt, that caused the USGA to get rid of 36-hole finishes at the U.S. Open. Same for the elimination of the 18-hole playoff in The Masters and the British Open. In 1935, for example, when Gene Sarazen hit the famous double eagle at the 15th hole, he and Craig Wood went an extra 18 holes. Tied again, they went another 18. In effect, then, we've gone from 36 extra holes to sudden death. Securing good ratings on Sunday afternoon is a high priority. No network wants to end play on a Monday, when people (consumers) are at work. I see the point, but, to me, television should adapt to the game, not the other way around.

The money, I also contend, has changed the players. When I was playing, there were true originals, such as Jimmy Demaret, Tommy Bolt, Jackie Burke, and Lloyd Mangrum. We also had our share of original swings, some of which weren't so pretty, which is what made them so original. Today, check out the driving range of any PGA Tour event, and you may have a difficult time distinguishing one player from the next. They look much the same, and their swings are very similar. It's almost as if they enrolled in a course and don't dare to deviate from the blueprint. It's a good thing, I suppose, that they put the players' names on boards behind them.

The money also allows players to skip certain tournaments to prepare for the ones with larger purses, creating, in essence, a two-tier system on the tour. As a consequence, events that don't attract the bigger names suffer. I would be in favor of requiring that each player compete in a specific tournament at least once every four years. We should do whatever is possible to help these neglected tournaments. These tournaments were once the tour's backbone.

So far, I believe, the game has survived pretty well, and a big part of that is because of star power—people like Walter Hagen, Chi Chi Rodriguez, Fuzzy Zoeller, and Lee Trevino, who have not been just outstanding golfers. They have also been entertainers, keenly aware that people are interested in seeing more than good scores. That will never change. Yet, as I evaluate the current crop of promising players, I don't see many entertainers. I see very serious young men who seem unwilling to stand out from the crowd.

Why is this happening? For starters, they don't want to say or do the wrong thing, risking the clean image they need to secure endorsement dollars. For another, they grew up in country clubs and college campuses, exposed, in most cases, to a very narrow environment. They didn't grow up on municipal courses or work as caddies, like the players in my generation, who learned about life, as well as about golf. Some teenagers today enroll in special golf academies, another refuge from the real world.

Such pampering, in my opinion, will hinder many of these players in the long run. At some point, they will encounter adversity, both on and off the course. How will they react then? Will they possess the mental toughness to overcome it? I'm not so sure. They've never had to overcome adversity before.

The loss of the caddie at country clubs also concerns me. I wonder if we may be headed for a day when they might be extinct. I really hope not. I'm not totally opposed to the use of carts. We need them, but the caddie has long been one of golf's greatest traditions, and it must be maintained. I started as a caddie and wouldn't have had it any other way. It gave me a love for the game and a respect for the proper way to play it. Sadly, carts have become necessary on many of the modern courses, which, too difficult to navigate on foot, are designed with the purpose of selling real-estate plots. A lot of good caddies can't find work.

I also don't believe today's tour players have the fun we did. They don't hang around so much with each other away from the golf course. They hang around with their agents, their trainers, the people who are on the payroll. They treat golf as a business more than a game.

Believe me, the game of golf is in good hands, growing at a rate many could never have anticipated. I am impressed by its popularity in Europe and Asia, and how well foreign players have done here, especially on the LPGA Tour. I think this is a wonderful development. To see the game's inherent values reach people in faraway lands can only bring everyone closer together.

I also support the goals of the First Tee program, the effort to introduce golf into America's inner cities. I only hope that there will be sufficient follow-up. It would be a shame to get youngsters excited about the game but fail to provide them with a place to play.

During the growth in the years ahead, we must always be vigilant about preserving the game's traditions. Every time there's change of any kind, I reflect back to Jones, Hogan, and Sarazen, and I ask myself: is this something they would endorse?

I'm not opposed to all change. I recognize that each generation must leave its mark on the game.

But let's take it more slowly, and let's not turn our back on the past.

Chapter Twenty

WHY ME?

There are moments when my mind wanders, when I imagine what I could have accomplished if . . .

If there had been no car accident in Cleveland.

If I had won The Masters in 1956, 1958, or 1960.

If I hadn't lost the feeling in my hands.

How many tournaments could I have won? How many records could I have set? I'm not suggesting I would have been as good as a Ben Hogan or a Byron Nelson or a Sam Snead or a Jack Nicklaus, but I think it's safe to speculate that I would have put up some impressive numbers of my own. By the age of 33, I had already captured 13 tournaments. I was just entering my prime, both physically and mentally. There was nothing to keep me from fulfilling my expectations. But speculation is all it is and all it will ever be.

Am I bitter about the missed opportunities? Absolutely not. The way I look at it, I feel the exact opposite. I don't know of anyone in the history of the game who has been more fortunate, and that includes the long list of distinguished players who have won more tournaments and earned more money. I found love twice and friendships that have meant a lot more than any trophies. I found a new career, which afforded me a relationship with the public that I deeply value. I often wonder: why me? Why have *I* been so blessed? During an awards ceremony at the Waldorf Astoria, Jack Whitaker put it best: "Fate has a way of bending the twig and fashioning a man to his better instincts."

Why did Byron Nelson tutor me and give me all of his knowledge? What made me any more privileged than other promising young players? Tom Watson and I, in fact, are the only two players in 50 years who received such preferential treatment from Nelson. He was under no obligation, and asked for nothing in return. The three days I spent with him at the San Francisco Golf Club in the late summer of 1952 changed my life. I learned how to really play the game, understand its nuances, its temptations, its dangers, and love it more than ever. But, more important, I developed a profound respect for what the game truly represents. In the half century since, I have never met a finer gentleman than Byron Nelson, and I never will. He has been a second father to me.

Why did Ben Hogan take me under his wing? He wasn't someone in search of companionship. He was in search of perfection, and he came as close as anyone to achieving it. Yet Hogan gave me his time, and his wisdom, also without any conditions. I saw Hogan's strengths, and I saw his weaknesses, and both made me a better golfer and a better man. I was proud to call him my friend. With Nelson and Hogan in my corner, I felt like an apprentice painter who was taught by Michelangelo and shown by da Vinci.

Why did Gene Sarazen allow me to get so close? Sarazen was almost 30 years older, yet he treated me as a peer. His stories made a golden era come alive, with a magic that one can't possibly duplicate in the history books. I hope that, to some small degree, I've done the same for players 30 years younger than I am. I feel it is my responsibility, one that needs to be passed on through the generations.

My life in golf opened doors to many other worlds, as well. I got to know Frank Sinatra, the Sinatra away from the spotlight: a warm, sensitive man who couldn't bear to see other people in misery. He personified class and dignity, and I miss him dearly. I got to know Bing Crosby and Dean Martin and Joe DiMaggio. I got to know the most charismatic, talented entertainers of my generation.

I was blessed to meet presidents and other influential people in government. I played golf with Presidents Eisenhower, Nixon, Ford, and the elder Bush. In these gifted, fearless men, I learned about the leadership skills that have helped to keep this country great.

I was blessed to have parents who sacrificed so much. They loved me, nurtured me, and, perhaps most important, believed in me, even when I didn't. They never let me take the easy way out, knowing the easy way was often the wrong way. When my dad told me days before my hand operation in 1970 that I was the best golfer he ever saw, I knew I could face anything.

I have been blessed for what I learned about myself. When the speech therapist warned my mother I would be an "incurable stammerer" for the rest of my life, I decided to fight back. Learning how to play golf was a first step. But there was no way to really know if fighting back would be enough. Nobody truly knows until they try. Were there times when I felt like giving up? Of course. But, each time, I tapped into a powerful force inside

GETTING UP & DOWN

me I could never describe. I tapped into that force my whole life, after losing tournaments, after losing loved ones, after losing everything that mattered.

I felt it when I decided to turn pro, giving up a secure job in Eddie Lowery's automobile dealership in an attempt to prove myself against the best players in the world. I knew, despite the 80 at Augusta National in 1956, that I was no choker, and I knew there was only one way to prove it.

I felt it when I received the stern lecture from bartender Dave Marcelli. The next morning, I was hitting balls at California Golf Club. I wouldn't have another drink until I won again.

And I felt it when I dropped to my knees and prayed in my basement, when I finally summoned the courage to take a deep look, deeper than I ever dared to look, and didn't like what I saw. Either I was going to turn things around, or there was little chance they would ever turn around again. It was up to me and nobody else.

I've received numerous supportive letters and telegrams over the years from some fairly prominent people, and I cherish them all. But there is none I cherish as much as the letter I received in the late sixties from someone not so famous, a man I had never met.

Dear Mr. Venturi,

I would just like to take this opportunity to tell you what a difference you have made in my life. I'm a very successful man, have a wonderful family and children, and I'm on top of the world, and I owe it all to you. When you won the Open in 1964, I was in my car. I pulled to the side of the road near the Presidio. I wasn't on top of the world. I was, actually, on my way to commit suicide by jumping off the Golden Gate

Bridge. I listened to your story on the radio, and I said to myself, "If Ken Venturi can come back from so much adversity, well, so can I." Thank you very much for saving my life.

On the subject of saving lives, I have my own group of people to thank. I was feeling lost until I met Beau. My career and marriage were both going nowhere, and there was nothing to take their place. But this small lady with a huge heart made me see possibilities I never saw before. I can't imagine how my life would have gone without her. Why me? Why was I so blessed? I feel the exact same way about Kathleen. She made me see other possibilities, that a life after Beau—and, eventually, after CBS—could still be a full and meaningful one.

I have tried to give back as much as I could, to follow through on what I promised God that morning in my basement 40 years ago. Helping a blind person find a dog or helping an abused woman find a home has meant so much to me. I understand now why giving is more important than receiving.

On most mornings, I'm on the practice tee by about 6:30. I go immediately to the far end, where I hit balls for about 90 minutes. I am always by myself.

I don't practice because I'm preparing for a golf tournament. I rarely, in fact, play 18 holes. I've posted enough scores in my lifetime. Besides, people would expect to see the 1964 Open champion, and I don't play like the 1964 Open champion.

I hit balls because I love it as much as ever, just as I love to sit in my garage, fixing my clubs, listening to Sinatra. That will never change.

One recent morning, everything clicked. For weeks, I had been working on lengthening my swing, trying to compensate again for my bad hands. I wasn't making as much headway as I had hoped.

Suddenly, I was hitting the ball 260 yards and straight. A few of the shots reminded me of ones I hit 40, maybe 50, years ago. I can picture the hole, the shot, the circumstances—the moments frozen in my mind.

There are many other moments I can picture: hitting balls at Harding Park. Walking down the fairways with Nelson or Hogan. Soaking up the applause at Congressional. Sharing a laugh with Sinatra, a cry with my loved ones. I wouldn't trade my life with anyone. Again, I ask: oh, Lord, why me?

INDEX